First World War

and Army of Occupation

War Diary

France, Belgium and Germany

58 DIVISION
174 Infantry Brigade
London Regiment
2/8 Battalion
26 January 1917 - 28 February 1918

WO95/3006/3

The Naval & Military Press Ltd
www.nmarchive.com
Published in association with The National Archives

Published by

The Naval & Military Press Ltd

Unit 10 Ridgewood Industrial Park,

Uckfield, East Sussex,

TN22 5QE England

Tel: +44 (0) 1825 749494

www.naval-military-press.com

www.nmarchive.com

This diary has been reprinted in facsimile from the original. Any imperfections are inevitably reproduced and the quality may fall short of modern type and cartographic standards.

Contents

Miscellaneous	2/8th Bn. The London Regiment Special O.O.		
Miscellaneous	Reference Para 5 Of 174th Inf Bde Order No. 44	09/09/1917	09/09/1917
Miscellaneous	Patrols		
Miscellaneous	Report On Minor Enterprise By 2/8th Bn. London Regt. Carried Out On Night	10/09/1917	10/09/1917
Miscellaneous	2/8th Bn. The London Regiment Special O.O		
Operation(al) Order(s)	2/8th Battalion London Regiment Operation Order No.6	18/09/1917	18/09/1917
Miscellaneous			
Miscellaneous	2/8th Battalion London Regiment Report on Operations of 20th September 1917 Alberta Section (Ypres)	25/09/1917	25/09/1917
War Diary	Landrethun	01/10/1917	14/10/1917
War Diary	Poperinghe	20/10/1917	23/10/1917
War Diary	Siege Camp	24/10/1917	25/10/1917
War Diary	Canal Bank	26/10/1917	26/10/1917
War Diary	Ypres	29/10/1917	29/10/1917
War Diary	V.19.a.7.1.	30/10/1917	30/10/1917
War Diary	Seige Camp	31/10/1917	31/10/1917
Miscellaneous	The Following Awards Were Made After The Operations Of 20th Sept		
Diagram etc	Diagram		
Map	Map		
Operation(al) Order(s)	2/8th Bn. The London Regiment Operation Order No.7		
Miscellaneous	Preliminary Report On Operations	30/10/1917	30/10/1917
Miscellaneous	Administrative Instructions	28/10/1917	28/10/1917
War Diary	Siege Camp	01/11/1917	05/11/1917
War Diary	Canal Bank	06/11/1917	06/11/1917
War Diary	Ypres	08/11/1917	12/11/1917
War Diary	Siege Camp	15/11/1917	15/11/1917
War Diary	Herzeele	17/11/1917	24/11/1917
War Diary	Proven	25/11/1917	25/11/1917
War Diary	Seninghem	26/11/1917	26/11/1917
War Diary	Arlette	27/11/1917	28/11/1917
War Diary	Escoeuilles	29/11/1917	05/12/1917
War Diary	Bayengham	07/12/1917	08/12/1917
War Diary	Kempton Park	08/12/1917	09/12/1917
War Diary	In The Line	10/12/1917	12/12/1917
War Diary	Canal Bank	13/12/1917	08/01/1918
War Diary	Road Camp	08/01/1918	20/01/1918
War Diary	Moreuil	20/01/1918	30/01/1918
War Diary	Hangard	30/01/1918	30/01/1918
Operation(al) Order(s)	2/8th Bn. London Regt. Order No.8	07/01/1918	07/01/1918
Miscellaneous	Administrative Instructions In Connection With Order No.8	07/01/1918	07/01/1918
Miscellaneous	Os.C. Companies Headquarters.	15/01/1918	15/01/1918
Miscellaneous	Administrative Instructions No.		
Miscellaneous	Transport Orders In Connection Administrative Instructions No. 9 For Move To Fifth Army	17/01/1918	17/01/1918
Operation(al) Order(s)	2/8th Bn. The London Regiment Order No.9	18/01/1918	18/01/1918
Operation(al) Order(s)	2/8th London Regt. Order No. 10	29/01/1918	29/01/1918
Miscellaneous	Administrative Orders In Connection With Order No.10	29/01/1918	29/01/1918
War Diary	Hangard	01/02/1918	08/02/1918
War Diary	Pierremande	09/02/1918	09/02/1918
War Diary	Barisis	09/02/1918	28/02/1918
Map	Map		

58 DIVISION

174 BRIGADE

2/8 BN LONDON REGIMENT

1915 SEPT – 1916 FEB

1917 JAN – 1918 JAN

ABSORBED BY 1/8 BN
FEB 18

CONFIDENTIAL

Instructions regarding War Diaries and Intelligence Summaries are contained in F. S. Regs., Part II. and the Staff Manual respectively. Title pages will be prepared in manuscript.

WAR DIARY of 2nd Battn P.O.RIFLES

~~or INTELLIGENCE~~ SUMMARY.

(Erase heading not required.)

From Jan 26th 1917 to Jan 31st 1917

(VOLUME I)

Army Form C. 2118.

Place	Date	Hour	Summary of Events and Information	Remarks and references to Appendices
1917				
SUTTON VENY	Jan 26	11.45am	20 Officers + 521 Other Ranks left WARMINSTER HWP	
	27	11.30am	20 Officers, 525 O.R arrived at HAVRE. (3 LTMB + 1 174th Bde Batman joined at S'HAMPTON) HWP	
	28	3.17pm	20 Officers 523 O.R left HAVRE (1 Cook joining rear party of 174th Bde + 1 O.R. Sergt left at D.A.G's Office at HAVRE) HWP	
	30	12.15am	20 Officers 523 O.R arrived VILLERS L'HOPITAL + went into Billets. HWP	
		3.30pm	3 174th LTMB + 1 174th Bde Batman despatched to 174th Inf Bde HQ. HWP	

T2134. Wt. W708—776. 500000. 4/15. Sir J. C. & S.

Confidential

Instructions regarding War Diaries and Intelligence Summaries are contained in F. S. Regs., Part II. and the Staff Manual respectively. Title pages will be prepared in manuscript.

WAR DIARY
or
~~INTELLIGENCE~~ SUMMARY.
(Erase heading not required.)

2nd Bn Post Office Rifles
Feb 1st – 25th 1917
Vol 1

Army Form C. 2118.

Place	Date	Hour	Summary of Events and Information	Remarks and references to Appendices
VILLA L'Hopital	Feb 5	12 30	Orders received for Battn to move to POMMERA	MHP
POMMERA	6	2pm	B Coy joined the Battn from England	MHP
"		8 pm	A Coy ditto	MHP
"	8	12 30pm	Orders received for Bn to move to Souastre & Transport to HENU	MHP
SOUASTRE		4.30pm	C & D Coys went into the Trenches for instruction under orders of 139th Bde	MHP
		5 pm	HQ A & B Coys ditto 138th Bde	MHP
	10	2-5pm	HQ, 2 platoons of A Coy & B Coy went into Billets at St AMAND	MHP
	11	4.30pm	Two platoons of A Coy relieved the other 2 platoons of A Coy in the Trenches	MHP
	12	3 30pm	B Coy went into Trenches as a Coy. Two platoons of A Coy returned to St AMAND	MHP
	13	6 pm	The whole Bn went by Lorries to POMMERA	MHP
	19	2pm	The Bn left POMMERA for HUMBERCAMP & arrived between 4.30pm & 6pm.	MHP
	20	8pm	The Battn proceeded by platoons to the trenches & it relieved the 8th West Yorks in C2.	MHP
	24	11.10pm	The Battn was relieved by 2/6th Bn Londons. The Line was quiet & no casualties occurred.	MHP

T2134. Wt. W708–776. 500000. 4/15. Sir J. C. & S.

Confidential

Instructions regarding War Diaries and Intelligence Summaries are contained in F. S. Regs., Part II. and the Staff Manual respectively. Title pages will be prepared in manuscript.

WAR DIARY or ~~INTELLIGENCE SUMMARY.~~

(Erase heading not required.)

2/8 London Regt

2nd Battn P.O.Rifles

FROM Feb 26th to March 25th 1917

Volume I

Army Form C. 2118.

Vol 3

Place	Date	Hour	Summary of Events and Information	Remarks and references to Appendices
Trenches	Feb 28	9.15pm	The Battalion relieved 2/6th Battalion	H&P
	March 3		Our trenches were heavily shelled from 12.15pm onwards. 2909 Rfn Wren wounded	H&P
	" 4	3.45pm	Battalion was relieved by 2/6th Battn + went to BAILLEULMONT. 3 Casualties 3239 L/cpl Johnson H, Shell shocked	H&P
			3353 Rfn Bushel, FG wounded at duty, 3568 Rfn Hennessey. P. wounded at duty.	H&P
	" 5		Two casualties from shell fire [5218 Rfn Fitzpatrick killed 3323 L/cpl Lowry wounded at duty, in BAILLEULMONT	H&P
	" 6		2218 Sgt Read killed by shell in BAILLEULMONT	H&P
	" 17	8 am	Battalion relieved 2/7th Battn London in Right Sector.	H&P
		1.30pm	2Lt Tregelles + an RA Officer suspecting the Boche to have evacuated his trenches went over to his lines + found it evacuated	H&P
		2.30pm	Lt Tregelles and 9 O.R. proceeded to reconnoitre MONCHY + entered ADINFER WOOD returning to Coy H.Q. at 6.30pm. No enemy was seen. Major de Vesian also reconnoitred MONCHY	H&P
	" 18	12.15am	Orders were received from Bde to send one Coy to enter + occupy RANSART if possible. C Coy under Capt P.C.M. Ash entered RANSART + reported it clear of enemy at 5.40.am.	H&P
		11.40am	Orders received to withdraw Coys when covered + move to BAILLEUVAL which was reached at 6.30pm	H&P
			Three casualties. 3219 Rfn Mason CH wounded by kicking a bomb in No mans land. 5157 Rfn Gray slightly wounded from same bomb. 2912 Cpl Burgess wounded by bomb picked up by a trained bomber	H&P

T2131. Wt. W708—776. 500000. 4/15. Sir J. C. & S.

Confidential

Instructions regarding War Diaries and Intelligence Summaries are contained in F. S. Regs., Part II. and the Staff Manual respectively. Title pages will be prepared in manuscript.

WAR DIARY
or
~~INTELLIGENCE~~ SUMMARY.
(Erase heading not required.)

2nd Battn P.O. Rifles
FROM Feb 26th to March 25th 1917
Volume I

Army Form C. 2118.

Place	Date	Hour	Summary of Events and Information	Remarks and references to Appendices
			who failed to throw the bomb clear.	HCP
BAILLEVAL	March 19	8.40	Orders received that Bn was under the orders of the C.R.E. & was to proceed to billets at BRETENCOURT	HCP
			which was reached at 4 pm.	HCP
	20	2 am	Orders received from Bde that Battn was to move to BERLES which was reached at 6.15 pm.	HCP
	21		Orders were received to go to BIENVILLERS on March 22nd	HCP
	22	8 am	Battalion proceeded to BIENVILLERS	HCP
	23	4.30 pm	Orders received from Bde to Relieve 2/6th Bn at BOIRY-STE-RICTRUDE on March 25	HCP
	24	5 pm	Above order Cancelled by Telegram from Bde	HCP.

T2134. Wt. W708—776. 500000. 4/15. Sir J. C. & S.

Instructions regarding War Diaries and Intelligence Summaries are contained in F. S. Regs., Part II. and the Staff Manual respectively. Title pages will be prepared in manuscript.

WAR DIARY
or
~~INTELLIGENCE~~ ~~SUMMARY.~~
(Erase heading not required.)

Army Form C. 2118.

2nd Battn P.O. Rifles 2/8 London R[?]
From March 26th - April 25th 1917
Vol I

Vol 4

Place	Date	Hour	Summary of Events and Information	Remarks and references to Appendices
BIENVILLERS	March 24th	6pm	The following Officers reported for duty:- Major A MAXWELL. D.S.O. 2/Lieut H.W. Leask, 2/Lieut F.S. Mortimer.]	HWP
	27	2pm	C+D Coys proceeded to BOISLEUX AU MONT for work on Railway under 19th Coy French Engineers.	HWP
	April 3rd	7.30am	Battalion less C+D Coys left BIENVILLERS for SOUASTRE	HWP
		6.30pm	C+D Coys joined Battalion at SOUASTRE.	HWP
	March 29		2/Lieut R.A. Keene proceeded to 58th Div Depot Battalion	HWP
	30		Lieut W.A. Stirling proceeded to Training Base depot HAVRE.	HWP
			Lieut C.A. Montgomery attd to 174th Bde as Intelligence Officer	HWP
	April 4	7pm	Battalion arrived at LYTHAM CAMP MAILLY-MAILLET	HWP
MAILLY-MAILLET	5		Nine O.R. reported as Reinforcement.	HWP
	7	4.30pm	Battalion moved into Camp near BIHUCOURT [G.13.c.9.4]	HWP
BIHUCOURT			Capt G.C. Faber evacuated to England Sick	HWP
	13		Major A MAXWELL proceed to 1/8th Battn LONDON Regt	HWP
	18		374022 Rfn HENLEY G.J. C Coy wounded (slightly in shoulder) at Duty. } Working on L'COURT-MORY Rd	HWP
	20		371033 L/Cpl DUNLOP A B Coy wounded (Shell wound in thigh) }	HWP
			372503 Rfn WILKES L A Coy wounded (Shell wound in back) }	HWP
			371280 Rfn COOPER G G A Coy wounded (Shell wound in left arm) }	HWP

T2134. Wt. W708-776. 500000. 4/15. Sir J. C. & S.

Instructions regarding War Diaries and Intelligence Summaries are contained in F. S. Regs., Part II. and the Staff Manual respectively. Title pages will be prepared in manuscript.

WAR DIARY
or
~~INTELLIGENCE~~ SUMMARY.
(Erase heading not required.)

Army Form C. 2118.

2nd Battalion PO Rifles
From March 26th - April 25th (Continued)
Vol I

Place	Date	Hour	Summary of Events and Information	Remarks and references to Appendices
DIHUCOURT	Apr 20		371087 L/cpl Tysall A T D Coy 'Shell Shocked' returned to Battn April 22nd	HWP
		4pm	Capt J A WEBSTER proceeded to H.Q Div General of Transportation.	HWP
	23	4 pm	Eight Other Ranks joined Battalion as reinforcement.	HWP

Hugh W Whelley Capt & Adjt
2/8th Battn London Regt

T2131. Wt. W708—776. 500000. 4/15. Sir J. C. & S.

War Diary

of

2/8 Ldn. Regt.

(P.O.R)

From 26.3.17

to 25.4.17

Ref: ECOUST 2/8th Bn., ORDER No: 8. Copy No: 1
ST-MEIN map.
Edition 3.

WAR DIARY APPENDIX I

1. The battalion will relieve the Infantry in BULLECOURT tonight.

2. C. Company will take approximately from the left of the 173 Bde to U.[illegible].c.[illegible].
   D. Company thence to U.[illegible].a.00.[illegible].
   A. Company thence to approx. [illegible].
   Each company will have 1 platoon in support.
   B. Company in reserve from U.[illegible].a.[illegible].10. to U.[illegible].
   Battalion H.Q. at [illegible].10.
   R.A.P. at [illegible].
   The M.O. and reserve S.B.s. will move with Bn. H.Q. and return with relieved troops to R.A.P.

3. Companies will move at [illegible] paces between platoons so as to be at the WINDMILL [illegible], where Company guides will meet them as follows:
   C. Co. 9.15. pm.
   D. Co. 9.45. pm.
   A. Co. 10.15. pm.
   B. Co. 10.45. pm.
   Bn.H.Q. 10.45. pm.

4. The relief will proceed by the communicating trench beginning at C.3.a.10.30. Pace along trench must not exceed 2 miles per hour. No interval between platoons in trench.

5. Platoon guides will meet platoons at end of com. trench near crater ~~xxxxxxx~~ at point 51.

6. All platoons and H.Q. will arrange for gas gong alarms and sentries.

7. Pack ponies with petrol tins full of water will be at the crater at C.[illegible].a.00.20. at [illegible].20. pm. (see para 10.)

8. Limbers with L.G.s. will accompany companies as far as possible. The battalion tools will be dumped by Transport at the WINDMILL and carried by platoons so that each platoon has 8 shovels and 4 picks.

9. Each company commander must have Very pistols with white and red cartridges and a full complement of trench store.

10. The Water tins will be carried up by a carrying of another battalion to Bn. H.Q. where it will be kept in reserve and issued to companies equally.

11. Every care must be taken to conceal the relief movement and trench position.

12. The semicircular line of the road constituting the front must be held at all costs.

13. Every effort should be made to improve cover tonight and to clean the ground, bury dead, and collect salvage as soon as possible.

14. Listening posts and patrols must be constantly employed to detect enemy movements.

15. Special instructions will be issued about reports.

16. These orders will be destroyed before going into the trenches.

BY ORDER.

Copy No: 1 War Diary.
2 A. Co.
3 B. Co.
4 C. Co.
5 M.O.
6 T.O.
7 Bde. H.Q.
8 H.Q.

Vol 5

CONFIDENTIAL

****

W A R   D I A R Y

OF

2/8th Bn London Regt

From 27/4/17

To 25/5/17

Instructions regarding War Diaries and Intelligence Summaries are contained in F. S. Regs., Part II. and the Staff Manual respectively. Title pages will be prepared in manuscript.

WAR DIARY
or
~~INTELLIGENCE SUMMARY.~~ 2nd Battn P.O. Rifles from April 26th to May 25th
Vol I

(Erase heading not required.)

Army Form [illegible]2118.

Place	Date	Hour	Summary of Events and Information	Remarks and references to Appendices
BIHUCOURT	April 27		2/Lt C.E. Collings and 2/Lt L.J. Wakefield joined from Base. HWP	
	28		Capt M.F. Buckdale wounded on working party HWP	
	May 6		Capt Webster rejoined. HWP	
	7		2/Lt Stroud joined from Base. HWP	
	14	2pm	Battn moved to Camp at MORY B28.a.15.70. HWP	
		7.15pm	Coy Officers proceeded to BULLECOURT preparatory to taking over the Line. HWP	
	15		Capt P.F. Wheeldon + Sergt Moore wounded. HWP	
		7.45pm	Battalion moved off to take over trenches in BULLECOURT from a composite Battn of 7th Division as per orders marked appendix I HWP	See appendix I
			Positions of Coys as taken over are shown on attached Map marked appendix II. A Coy in Blue, HWP D Coy in Green, C Coy in Brown, B Coy in pencil - the final position of A Coy after the attack on May 17th is shown in Red. HWP	" II
			~~[illegible]~~ The incidents in the tour of duty + the attack delivered at 2 am on HWP May 17th on the N.W. portion of BULLECOURT are all contained in appendix III. HWP	III
			Casualties 3 Officers (Capt Wheeldon wounded on May 15th whilst reconnoitring, Capt Stapylton HWP + 2/Lt Collings shell shocked on May 16th) HWP	

T2134. Wt. W708—776. 500000. 4/15. Sir J. C. & S.

Instructions regarding War Diaries and Intelligence Summaries are contained in F. S. Regs., Part II. and the Staff Manual respectively. Title pages will be prepared in manuscript.

WAR DIARY
or
~~INTELLIGENCE~~ SUMMARY. from April 26th to May 25th (Continued)

(Erase heading not required.)

Army Form C. 2118.

Place	Date	Hour	Summary of Events and Information		Remarks and references to Appendices
			OR Killed 7	HWP	
			Died of Wounds 3		
			Wounded 45		
			Shell Shock 5		
			60	HWP	
			All Shell Shock cases of OR + 5 wounded rejoined.	HWP	
			2/Lt Collings rejoined 20.5.17	HWP	
			A list of Officers that went up into the line with the Battn is attached as appendix V	HWP	See Appendix IV
	May 17th	4pm	Major de Vesian T.D. took over Command of Battn.	HWP	
	18th		Lt Col P.J. Preece went to England.	HWP	
	24th		2/Lt Bovett, R.D. joined for duty.	JCS	
			2/Lt Collinge went to convalescent camp. Hugh W. Chester, Capt & Adjt	JCS	
	25th		Battn moved up into support position on LONGATTE - NOREUIL ROAD	JCS	
			Geoffrey Charles [illegible]		

T2134. Wt. W708—776. 500000. 4/15. Sir J. C. & S.

Instructions regarding War Diaries and Intelligence Summaries are contained in F. S. Regs., Part II. and the Staff Manual respectively. Title pages will be prepared in manuscript.

WAR DIARY or ~~INTELLIGENCE~~ SUMMARY.

(Erase heading not required.)

2nd Battn P.O. Rifles
May 26 – June 30th
Vol I

Army Form C. 2118.

Place	Date	Hour	Summary of Events and Information	Remarks and references to Appendices
MORY	May 25	8.45	The Battn left MORY CAMP B 28a for BULLECOURT SECTOR ~~night~~ subsector Support to relieve 2/11 London Regt.	HoP
	26		The Battn was relieved by 2/5 London Regt + went to right subsector front line relieving 2/12th London Regt + remained there four days + suffered following casualties – 2/Lt F.M. SUTCLIFFE killed on May 29th	HoP
			OR killed 7. OR wounded 21.	HoP
	29		2/Lt G. Chancellor reported for duty.	HoP
			2/Lt T.W. Sloan ditto.	HoP
	30/31		Battn was relieved by 2/6th London Regt + went to Support at ECOUST	HoP
	30th		Lt Col A D Derviche-Jones M.C. reported for duty to Command vice Lt P.J. Preece.	HoP
	June 1		2/Lt D.A. STROUD wounded on carrying party. OR killed 3 OR wounded 8. all on working parties.	HoP
	2		Battn was relieved by 2/12 London Regt + returned to MORY CAMP.	HoP
			2/Lt R.H. Taylor reported for duty	HoP
	7	8.15pm	The Battn left MORY + relieved 2/3rd in St LEDGER Sector Right Subsector.	
			+ came under orders of 173rd Bde for 2 days. Casualties OR killed 1 OR wounded 2.	HoP
	8		2/Lt G.C. Bourne and 2/Lieut G. Gibbs to R.F.C. – 2/Lieut F.S. Mortimer to V Corps as Musketry Instructor.	
	10	1.30am	The Bn was relieved by 2/7th London + returned to MORY CAMP	HoP

APPENDIX 111.

REPORT ON OPERATIONS AT BULLECOURT

from May 16th to May 18th 1917.

Ref. T.S. No:341. "BULLECOURT DEFENCES 1/5,000

On the night of 15/16th May the Battalion took over the front line of the BULLECOURT Sector from the 20th Manchester Regiment and other details of the 7th Division.

Since the reconnaissance on the previous day the situation in BULLECOURT had been altered by a German counter-attack which was delivered on the night 14/15th May and drove our troops from that part of BULLECOURT lying west of the LONGATTE - BULLECOURT Road. The new line ran approximately as follows : - U 22 d.3010, - along road to BULLECOURT Church - cross roads U 27 b.7548 - U 27 b.8.2.

The Battalion left their Camp at MORY marching by companies beginning at 7.45.pm. Route across country to Windmill 500 yds due S of LONGATTE - C.T. leading from S.E. corner of ECOUST - thence led by guides to Bn.H.Q. at C 28.a.30.10

The dispositions of companies is shewn on map attached ; "C" & "D" Companies facing in a Northerly direction along the BULLECOURT - RIENCOURT road while "A" Company held a line running almost due south through the middle of the Village to a point in the original HINDENBURG line South of the Village (about U 27 b.80.15.) where they were separated from the enemy by a double block. The HINDENBURG line running N.W. from this point to the CRUCIFIX was known to be ocupied by the enemy, but it was not known in what strength it was held.

The position occupied by "C" Company consisted of a continuous trench.

"D" Company had 1 section of 13 platoon holding a detached trench at U 22 c.28.12., near the road junction; the ground held by 14 & 13 platoons(less 1 section) consisted of a continuous but roughly dug trench; No: 16 platoon held a strong point in course of construction near the Church; No: 15 a line of forward posts in shell holes.

"A" Company ~~xxxxx~~were in trenches and shell holes in the position shown on the map.

The relief was reported complete at 4.35.am on the 16th. The night/apart from intermittent shelling had been without incident, was employed in consolidation and patrolling. which

<u>16th May</u>

Our trenches and posts were shelled continuously during the day, but the work of consolidation was continued and many dead were buried.

During the day arrangements were made for "C" & "D" Coys. to cooperate with the 173rd Bde on our right who were about to attack and occupy that portion of the BOVIS Trench due North of the line occupied by "C" Company U 22 c.30.48 to U 22.c.90.35.

"C" Company were to protect the left flank of the advance and prevent the enemy from reinforcing either from the West along the trench or from the North down the road running S.S.W. from the FACTORY in U 22b.

It /

It had been previously ascertained by patrols sent out by "C" Company that the objective was held by the enemy in some strength.

"D" Company were to support "C" Company's left flank by placing a rifle grenade barrage on the enemy trench at U 22 c.20.50. at which point it was under observation from their right flank, and seen to be occupied.

These preparations were completed by 6. 0.pm. and at 6.30.pm the troops detailed by 173rd BDE advanced up the valley on the right of "C" Company, but they did not attack as had been arranged across the front of "C" Company and later in the evening it was found that the left of the 173rd Bde was in position in a trench due North of the right of our line. Touch with them was maintained by the establishment of two posts in the gap and by moving up No 5 platoon of "B" Company which remained at the disposal of O.C."C" Company.

The forward posts of the 173rd Bde were however withdrawn during the night and our line reestablished in its original position.

At 11. 0.pm. all Company Commanders were summoned to Bn.H.Q. to be informed as to the plan of an attack ordered to be delivered before dawn to clear the enemy from the Western half of the village.

The 2/5th (L.R.B.) from their position along the Railway Embankment S.W. of the village were at 2.am to attack in a N.N.E direction, their first objective being the German trench South of the village between the ECOUST - BULLECOURT and ECOUST - LONGATTE roads and their second the road running parallel thereto and just North of it.

"A" Company under 2/Lt Blane (Capt W.E.C. Staplyton having meantime become a casualty) were to cooperate as soon as the L.R.B. had attained their 2nd objective and advance North Westwards with a view to clearing the rest of the village and establishing posts bejond it. For this purpose they were, as soon as the L.R.B. had reached their second objective, to withdraw Nos 1 & 2 plateons and as a company in normal formation advance across the front of the L.R.B. from the line of the road running S.S.W. from the Church.

<u>17th May</u>

This plan was successfully carried out by about 3.30.am though not without great difficulty owing to the state of the ground which was pitted with shell holes and covered with debris.

During the advance of "A" Company patrols of "D" Company which had been echeloned in rear, advanced to protect their right front and afterwards occupied position facing Northwards until by posts of "A" Company then covered the whole of the Western half of the Village.

The position of these posts is shown on the map attached. During this advance thirteen prisoners were captured by "A" Company. Casualties see WAR DIARY

During the day the work of consolidation, especially of the new posts was continued in spite of the activity of the enemy's snipers who caused some casualties

Patrols/

Patrols were also sent out for the purpose of observing the enemy's line at U 22 c.20.50.

18th May

The Battalion was relieved by the 2/5th Battalion (L.R.B.) the relief being completed by 12.5.am. and withdrew to positions as follows :-

"B" Company to line of Railway from about U 27 d.20.40. to U 27 c.00.30.

H.Q., and "D" Company to ECOUST.

"A" & "C" Companies to dugouts in VAULX - VRAUCOURT - ST LEGER road N. of SUCRERIE in B 24.a & b.

The Battalion was relieved by the 2/7th Battalion but owing to working parties the relief could not be completed until 3. 0.am on May 19th.

The Battalion went into Camp at MORY at B 28 a.15.70.

APPENDIX 1V

LIST OF OFFICERS THAT WENT UP TO BULLECOURT ON MAY 15/16th 1917.

	Lt-Colonel P.J.Preece, T.D.	
	Major E de Vesian, T.D.	(May 17th)
	Capt & Adjutant H.W. Priestley.	
	Lt Shapley	
	2/Lt Mumford.	
	Capt R.D. Gawn (M.O.)	
"A" Company.	Capt W.E.C. Staplyton	(shell shock May 16th)
	Capt F.P. Wheeldon	(wounded May 15th)
	2/Lt A.F.W. Blande	
	2/Lt R.F. Tregelles.	
"B" Company.	2/Lt D.P. Pyke.	
	2/Lt Weiss	
"C" Company.	Major P.C.M. Ash.	(night of 14/15th only)
	2/Lt G.E. Gunning.	
	2/Lt Richardson	(attached to "B" Coy.)
	2/Lt E.R. Lanes	
	2/Lt Mortimer.	
"D" Company.	Major G.G. Barnes	
	Lt G.C. Bourne.	
	2/Lt C.E. Collinge	(shell shock May 16th)
	2/Lt G. Kelly.	

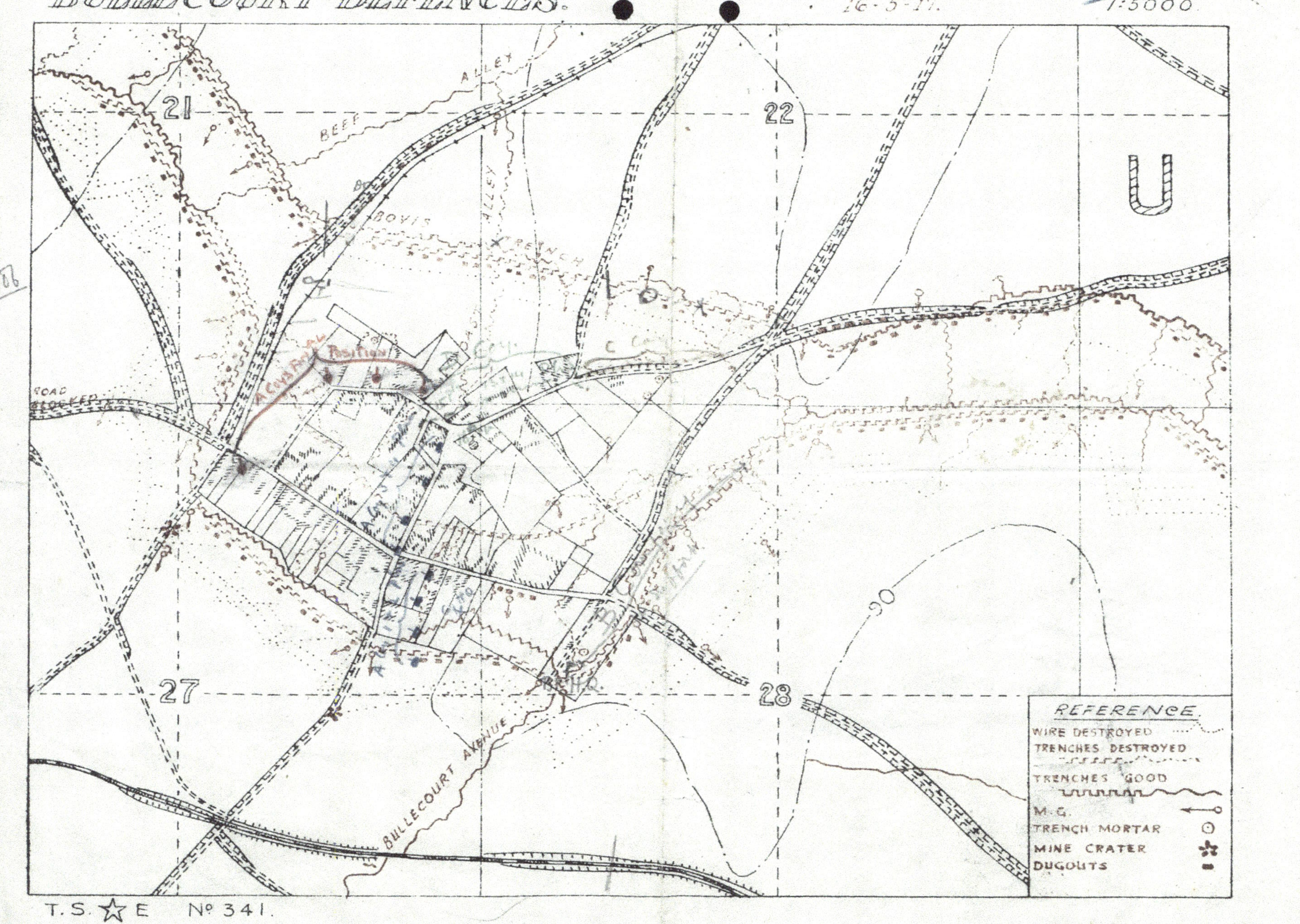
BULLECOURT DEFENCES.
16-5-17.
1:5000
21
22
27
28
U
BEEF ALLEY
BOVIS TRENCH
ALLEY
BULLECOURT AVENUE
ROAD
90
A Coys Final Position
REFERENCE.
WIRE DESTROYED
TRENCHES DESTROYED
TRENCHES GOOD
M.G.
TRENCH MORTAR
MINE CRATER
DUGOUTS
T.S. ☆ E No 341.

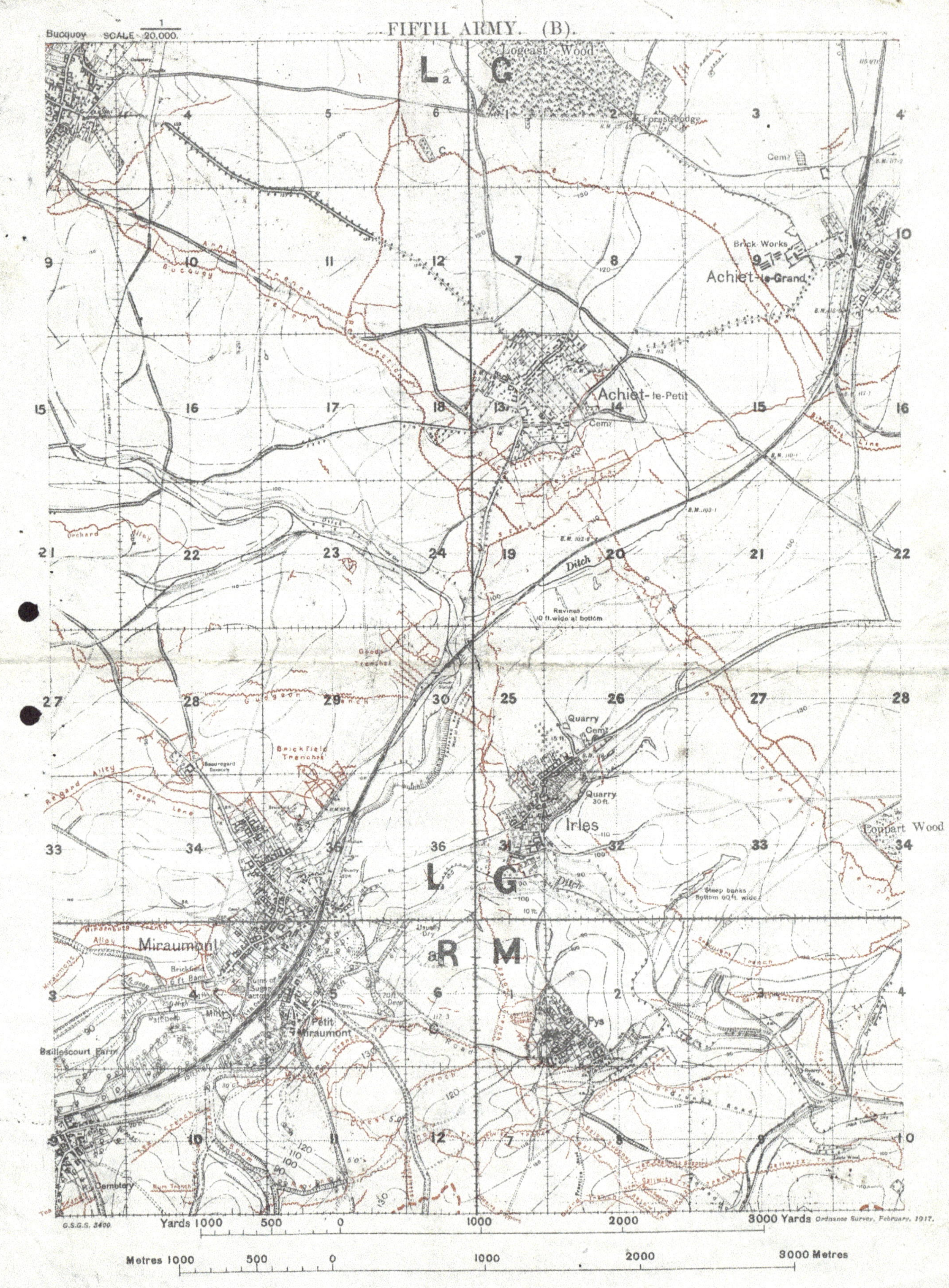
FIFTH ARMY. (B).
Bucquoy
SCALE 1/20,000.
Logeast Wood
Forest Lodge
Brick Works
Achiet-le-Grand
Achiet-le-Petit
Ravines 10 ft. wide at bottom
Ditch
Quarry
Cem.y
Brickfield Trenches
Beauregard Dovecot
Pigeon Lane
Irles
Loupart Wood
Steep banks bottom 60 ft. wide
Miraumont
Petit Miraumont
Pys
Baillescourt Farm
Cemetery
L a G
L G
a R M
Yards 1000 500 0 1000 2000 3000 Yards
Metres 1000 500 0 1000 2000 3000 Metres
G.S.G.S. 3400.
Ordnance Survey, February, 1917.

Confidential

Vol 6

War Diary

of

1/8th London Regt

from 25.5.17
to 30.6.17

2

Instructions regarding War Diaries and Intelligence Summaries are contained in F. S. Regs., Part II. and the Staff Manual respectively. Title pages will be prepared in manuscript.

WAR DIARY
or
~~INTELLIGENCE~~ SUMMARY.
(Erase heading not required.)

2nd Battn P.O. Rifles
May 26 – June 30th 1917
Vol [?]

Army Form C. 2118.

Place	Date	Hour	Summary of Events and Information	Remarks and references to Appendices
	June 13	8pm	Battalion left MORY CAMP + relieved 2/7th London. Strength Officers 19 OR 570.	HWP
			The line of posts taken over are shown on attd Map map appendix 'A' marked in blue.	APPENDIX A
	14/15		No 12 platoon led by 2Lieut Leask Jones in attack on HINDENBURG LINE made by 173rd Bde + No 9 platoon under 2Lieut Barnes had orders to link up the right of the captured Line with the left of our Right Coy posts (U20b 40.10 + U21c 05.40) These 2 platoons were to form a defensive flank on right of 173rd Bde Line.	
			The attack was launched at 2.15 am on June 15th. No 12 platoon gained its objective with the loss of 2Lt Leask (wounded) and 18 ORs wounded out of total 30 including 2 S.Bs. No 9 platoon took up position under enemy barrage which was put down within 4 minutes of ours commencing + formed four posts in the exposed road (U20.d 8.6) + in cutting connecting 173rd Bde's right + our left. Two of these posts were blown up with direct hits, lost heavily (8 killed and 12 wounded) and withdrew towards our right Coy. Our line of posts after the attack are shown in APPENDIX A marked in RED.	HWP
	15		Our new positions were shelled heavily during the day + communication with them was very difficult. At dusk the only communication between 173rd Bde Right + our left was by lamp.	HWP

T2134. Wt. W708–776. 500000. 4/15. Sir J. C. & S.

3

Instructions regarding War Diaries and Intelligence Summaries are contained in F. S. Regs., Part II. and the Staff Manual respectively. Title pages will be prepared in manuscript.

WAR DIARY
or
~~INTELLIGENCE~~ SUMMARY.
(Erase heading not required.)

2nd Battn P.O. Rifles
May 26 – June 30th 1917
Vol I

Army Form C. 2118.

Place	Date	Hour	Summary of Events and Information	Remarks and references to Appendices
		8.50pm	S.O.S by this lamp was picked up + forwarded to Bn HQ + thence to 173rd Bde.	
			Our barrage was put down simultaneously with enemy barrage. There is every reason to believe this foiled his Counter attack.	
	16		B Coy under 2/Lt D.P. PYKE was attached to 173rd Bde for their attack on HINDENBURG SUPPORT LINE being on the extreme right.	
			The attack was launched at 3.10 am + objective was partly gained with loss of 2/Lt PYKE (wounded) + 2/Lt L.J. WAKEFIELD (wounded + missing) OR killed 1, wounded 22, missing 1.	
			Those of B Coy who penetrated the enemies support line remained as part of the garrison of the 173rd Bde until they were relieved by 2/5th London Regt.	
	17		Posts were consolidated.	
	18		A volunteer party of 48 OR from B + D Coys under 2/Lt W.H. Richardson, Rev. G. Vernon-Smith + 2/Lt J.B. Weiss succeeded in bringing back 12 Stretcher + 4 walking cases from front line (about U 20 b 5.3) under Rifle + M.G. fire	
	15		Lt Col E de Vesian left to assume command of 1/8th Bn London Regt.	
	21		Communication Trench with left of BULLECOURT Garrison dug.	
			2/Lt J.B. Weiss to R.F.C.	

T2134. Wt. W708–776. 500000. 4/15. Sir J. C. & S.

4

Instructions regarding War Diaries and Intelligence Summaries are contained in F. S. Regs., Part II. and the Staff Manual respectively. Title pages will be prepared in manuscript.

WAR DIARY
or
~~INTELLIGENCE~~ SUMMARY.
(Erase heading not required.)

2nd Battn P.O. Rifles.
May 26 - June 30th 1917
Vol I

Army Form C. 2118.

Place	Date	Hour	Summary of Events and Information	Remarks and references to Appendices
	21		2/Lt G.H. Stevens + 2/Lt F.J. Edmonds joined for duty + stayed at Transport Lines	HWP
	23/24		Relieved by 22nd Manchesters + proceeded to MORY COPSE CAMP	
			Total Casualties (exclusive of those who rejoined from slight wounds) for tour	
			Officers 2 wounded 1 missing. O.R. Killed 13, Wounded 86, missing 4.	HWP
	24th		Battalion moves into Camp at COURCELLES.	
			2/Lt G. Cook joined for duty.	HWP
			Addenda — Leave of Officers during the Month.	
			CAPT H.W. PRIESTLEY — May 24th - June 5th	
			Capt J A WEBSTER — May 28 - June 9th	
			Lieut. T.A.B PURKIS — ditto.	
			Lieut R.N. SHAPLEY — June 8th - June 19th	
			Lt Col E de Vesian — May 31st - June 12th	
			Lieut A.D. HEATON — June 15th - June 26th	
			2/Lieut G.E. Gunning — June 20 - June 30th	
			2/Lieut E.R. Lanes — June 25th -	
			2/Lieut T.J. Mumford — June 29th - .	HWP

T2134. Wt. W708-776. 500000. 4/15. Sir J. C. & S.

6/

Instructions regarding War Diaries and Intelligence Summaries are contained in F. S. Regs., Part II. and the Staff Manual respectively. Title pages will be prepared in manuscript.

WAR DIARY
or
~~INTELLIGENCE SUMMARY.~~
(Erase heading not required.)

2nd Battn P.O. Rifles
May 25th – June 30th
Vol I.

Army Form C. 2118.

Place	Date	Hour	Summary of Events and Information	Remarks and references to Appendices
			The following recommendations for honours were made:-	
			Rev Guy Vernon-Smith recommended for M.C. & C.O	
			2/Lieut W. H. Richardson ditto	
			370601 Sergt. S. H DANIELS " M.M "	
			371371 L/cpl G. Solomon " DCM "	
			370124 Rfn W. E YOUNG " M M. "	
			371357 L/cpl R W CLAYTON " M M "	
			372654 Rfn C.W. Jefferson " M M. "	
			371219 L/cp LOWRY. " M M "	HOP

A. D. Derviche-Jones
[stamp:] LIEUT. COLONEL, COMMANDING 8TH (CITY OF LOND.) BATTN. POST OFFICE RIFLES.

T2134. Wt. W708—776. 500000. 4/15. Sir J. C. & S.

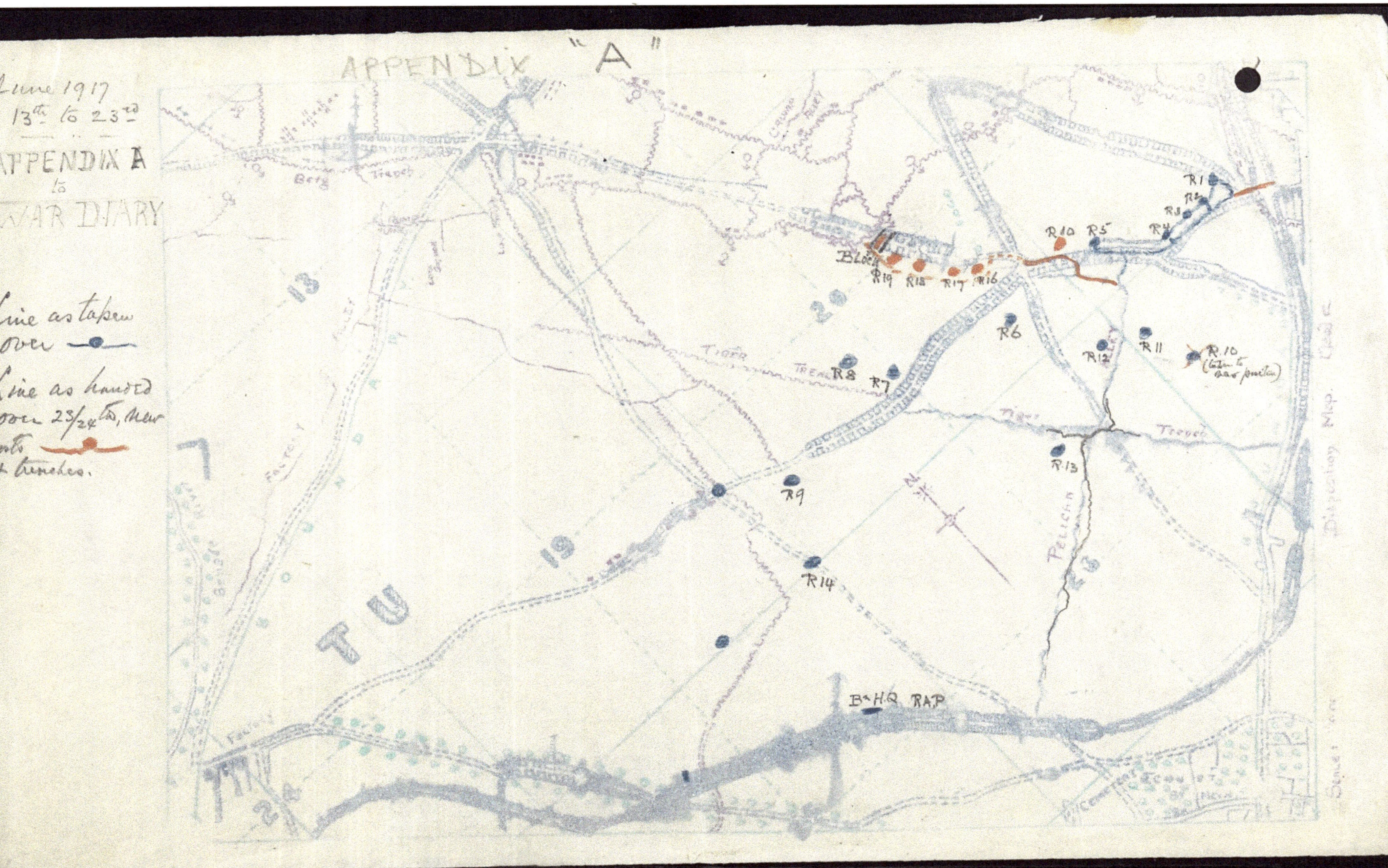
APPENDIX "A"
June 1917
13th to 23rd
APPENDIX A
to
WAR DIARY
Line as taken over
Line as handed over 23/24th, new posts & trenches.
R1
R2
R3
R4
R5
R6
R7
R8
R9
R10
R.10 (taken to new position)
R11
R12
R.13
R14
R16
R17
R18
R19
Block
Bn H.Q. RAP
Pelican
Tiger
Trench
Factory
Berg
Trench
TU
13
19
20
24

Instructions regarding War Diaries and Intelligence Summaries are contained in F. S. Regs., Part II. and the Staff Manual respectively. Title pages will be prepared in manuscript.

WAR DIARY
or
~~INTELLIGENCE SUMMARY.~~
(Erase heading not required.)

2nd Battn P.O. Rifles
July 1st – 31st
Vol II

2/8 London Regt
Vol 7

Army Form C. 2118.

Place	Date	Hour	Summary of Events and Information	Remarks and references to Appendices
COURCELLES	July 1		Ceremonial Parade – 372491 Rfn G H C Bass presented with Military Medal. – 2/Lieut T W Sloan proceeded on Musketry Course WARLOY. HWP	
	2		The following NCOs + Men were awarded the Military Medal. 371357 L/cpl Clayton RW 371219 L/cpl Lowry W, 372654 Rfn Jefferson CW, 370124 Rfn Young WE.	
			2/Lt ASW Blande proceeded to V Army Infantry School TOUTENCOURT. HWP	
	3		Lieut G.C. Gumming returned from Leave.	
	4	7pm	~~Inspection by G.O.C~~. Lt Col A.D. Derviche Jones + 2/Lt RF Tregelles proceeded on leave	
			Capt G.G. Barnes proceeded to England to Senior Officers Course Aldershot.	
			371371 L/cpl Solomon awarded Military Medal. HWP	
	5		Inspection by G.O.C Division. 2/Lieut S.R. Lanes returned from Leave. HWP	
	6	3.30pm	Battalion left COURCELLES + proceeded to Camp near BANCOURT by March Route HWP	
BANCOURT	7	3.30pm	Battalion left BANCOURT + proceeded by March Route to EQUANCOURT. HWP	
			Capt RD Gawn admitted to Hospital.	
EQUANCOURT	8		CO + Coy Commanders reconnoitred METZ area. HWP	
	9		2/Lts R.G. Barnes, R.D. Borrett + R.H. Taylor admitted to Hospital. HWP	
METZ	10	6am	Battalion left EQUANCOURT + took over Trenches as Brigade Reserve at METZ	

T2134. Wt. W708—776. 500000. 4/15. Sir J. C. & S.

Instructions regarding War Diaries and Intelligence Summaries are contained in F. S. Regs., Part II. and the Staff Manual respectively. Title pages will be prepared in manuscript.

WAR DIARY
or
~~INTELLIGENCE SUMMARY.~~
(Erase heading not required.)

2nd Battn P O Rifles
July 1st – 31
Vol II

Army Form C. 2118.

Place	Date	Hour	Summary of Events and Information	Remarks and references to Appendices
METZ	July 10		relieving 2/4 Leicester Regt. HWP	
			A Coy under Lt A D Heaton with 2/Lieut E R Lanes attd put at the disposal of 2/7th London Regt + took over DERBY Reserve trench. HWP	
	July 11		36 O R joined as reinforcements. HWP	
	12		2/Lieut T. J Mumford rejoined from leave. HWP	
	14		D Coy relieved A Coy in DERBY Reserve + came under orders of OC 2/7th London	
			A Coy reverting to Command of OC 2/8th Londons. HWP	
	16		D Coy reverted to Command of OC 2/8th London on being relieved by a Coy of 2/7th Londons HWP	
	17		Lt Col A.D. Derviche-Jones M C + 2/Lt R F Ingelles, returned from leave.	
			2/Lieut T W Sloan returned from Course.	
TRESCAULT Section	18	9.30pm	Battn left METZ to relieve part of 2/10th Londons in TRESCAULT – Map of trenches taken over as per map as shown in appendix 'A' HWP.	APPENDIX A
			Sgt Winship wounded in D Sap HWP	
	19		2/Lt R F Ingelles + 2 NCOs 13 Riflemen of A Coy left A Sap at Q 4 B 8.2 + after arriving at road at Q 4 B 8.7 turned N + followed Road on E side under a slight bank. Movement was heard in 'FEMY WOOD + on reaching K 35. C 0.3.	

Instructions regarding War Diaries and Intelligence Summaries are contained in F. S. Regs., Part II. and the Staff Manual respectively. Title pages will be prepared in manuscript.

WAR DIARY
or
~~INTELLIGENCE~~ SUMMARY.
(Erase heading not required.)

2nd Battn P.O. Rifles
July 1st – 31st
Vol II

Army Form C. 2118.

Place	Date	Hour	Summary of Events and Information	Remarks and references to Appendices
TRESCAULT Section	July		They were challenged by a German sentry located E of road. No shots were fired but many voices were heard + an enemy patrol 12 strong was seen coming from direction of FEMY WOOD to cut them off. Our patrol crawled back to Q4b.9.9. + went down road to point Q4B.7.3 + returned. The enemy appeared to be working in large numbers on a line K35.c.05 to K34 a 7.7 either wiring or digging. HWP	
	20		Lieuts Gunning, Richardson + Treggles all went on patrol + obtained valuable information	HWP
	21		2Lieut G.W. Chancellor rejoined from Course HWP	
			2Lieut T.M. MacBeth, 2Lieut R.B. Robinson + Hon Lt + QM. J. Gill joined for duty as reinforcements. HWP	
	22		2Lts Richardson + R.F. Treggles again obtained valuable information from patrolling. Rfn Green did not return from A Coys patrol + was reported missing.	HWP
	24		2Lieut Richardson + 6 men patrolled up to the enemies wire at the GLADE + saw 6 Germans at 20 yds distance. They covered them for 20 minutes hoping they would come close enough to secure but a Very Light disclosed their position + they opened fire + it is believed hit all six. HWP	

T2134. Wt. W708–776. 500000. 4/15. Sir J. C. & S.

4

Instructions regarding War Diaries and Intelligence Summaries are contained in F. S. Regs., Part II. and the Staff Manual respectively. Title pages will be prepared in manuscript.

WAR DIARY
or
~~INTELLIGENCE SUMMARY.~~
(Erase heading not required.)

2nd Battn P O Rifles
July 1 – 31st
Vol II

Army Form C. 2118.

Place	Date	Hour	Summary of Events and Information	Remarks and references to Appendices
TRESCAULT Section	July 25		96 OR joined as reinforcements. HWP	
	26	3pm	2Lieut G.H. Stephens & 2Lieut G. Cook were wounded by a shell which pitched on the top of B Coy H.Q. HWP	
	28/29		The Battalion was relieved by 2nd Battn S A Regt without incident & proceeded to NEUVILLE by Light Rly. HWP	APPx 'B'
NEUVILLE	29	6.30pm	The Battn formed up in NEUVILLE for Buses (which did not arrive until 7.15pm) to convey them to BAPAUME Station. HWP	"
		9.30pm	The Battn entrained at BAPAUME for BEAUMETZ which was reached at 2am July 30th. HWP	"
SIMENCOURT	30	3.40am	The Battn marched from BEAUMETZ into huts at SIMENCOURT HWP	"
	31		2Lieuts H. BOOTH, H. MOSS, C.H. WATSON, E.E.L TINSLEY & J.P.R SCRIVENER and 31 OR joined as reinforcements. HWP	

[illegible] Lt Col.
2/8th London R.

W708—776. 500000. 4/15. Sir J. C. & S.

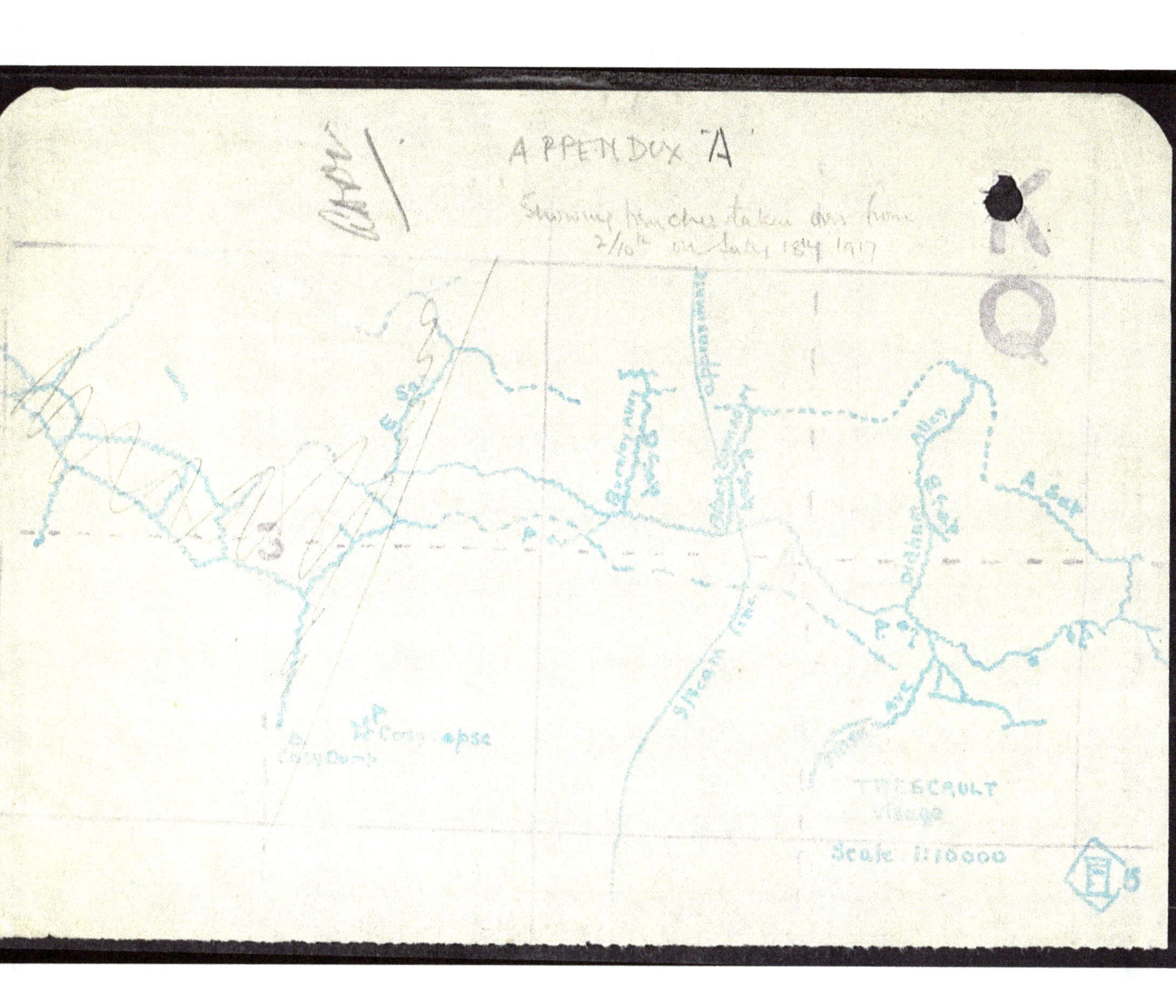
APPENDIX "A"
Showing trenches taken over from 2/10th on July 18th 1917
Scale 1:10000

SECRET. Copy No. 1...

ADMINISTRATIVE INSTRUCTIONS
in connection with Operation Order No. 20.

27th July, 1917.

1. The Battalion (less Transport) and 28 other ranks of Traffic Control will proceed to BAPAUME by bus on July 29th.
32 buses have been allotted which will leave NEUVILLE Cross Roads P.22.d.0.6. at 5 pm to catch No.4 Train which leaves BAPAUME at 10 pm.
Separate Orders for enbusing will be issued later.

2. The Transport Section will be divided as follows :-
(a) Entraining Portion
(b) Marching Portion.
The Entraining portion will be sub-divided as follows :-
Vehicles, etc. for No.1 Train.
4 Lewis Gun Limbers less Guns.
2 Cookers,
1 Mess Cart,
18 Chargers and Pack Animals,
1 Maltese Cart.
Vehicles for No. 2 Train.
2 Tool Limbers
2 Cookers
2 Water Carts.
The Marching Portion will consist of the remainder of the Transport, which will move on July 28th, halting and billeting at ABLAINZEVELLE for the night 28/29 continuing the march to SIMENCOURT on the 29th.
Lt. Purkis will be in charge and will receive special orders from Brigade.
Entraining Portion will leave FINS Camp by 4 pm on July 28th and will proceed to NEUVILLE Camp P.22.c.2.5.
Vehicles, etc. for No.1 Train will come under the ord rs of the B.T.O., and will proceed to BAPAUME passing the starting point Road Junction O.23.d.9.3. at 5.4 am on the 29th.
Vehicles for No.2 Train will come under the orders of an Officer of the 215th M.G.Coy., and will proceed to BAPAUME passing the same starting point at 11.34 am on the 29th.

3. (a) Details (excluding Transport) now at FINS Camp will move into Camp vacated by the 2nd S.A. Regt. NEUVILLEbon July 28th under orders to be issued by the Q.M.
(b) The party at present training at NEUVILLE will move into the same camp under orders to be issued by 2/Lt Mumford.

4. 2/Lt Mumford will report to the C.O. 2nd S.A.Regt. at NEUVILLE at 12 noon on July 28th and will make all arrangements for taking over the Camp finding guards, etc., and will detail the guides mentioned in para 6 of Operation Order No.20.

5. 2 Lorries (1½ for P.O.R. and ½ for 174th L.T.M.B.) have been allotted and will report to the Transport Lines FINS at 7 am on July 28th.
The Q.M. will see to the loading after which they will proceed direct to SIMENCOURT.

6. 2/Lt T.M. Sloan will act as entraining Officer at BAPAUME, and will report to Lt Wimble at BAPAUME Station at 8.45 am on July 29th.
He will receive from the Adjutant an entraining state shewing the number of this Battalion proceeding by each train.
He will leave BAPAUME by No.4 Train (vide Para 1).

7.

7. 2/Lt. R.F.Tregelles will act as detraining Officer at BEAUMETZ and will proceed there by No.3 Train leaving BAPAUME at 8 pm on July 29th.
He will report to Lt. Harrison Jones immediately on arrival at BEAUMETZ.

8. (a) Rations for the 28th and 29th will be drawn from the A.S.C. on the 27th.
Rations for the 28th will be delivered at Battn.H.Q. in the line by Transport in the usual way, and rations for the 29th except as in (b) will be taken under arrangements to be made by the Q.M. to NEUVILLE Camp and issued there.

(b) On the 27th the Q.M. will arrange to bring up to the line 2 days rations for the Officers and Other ranks staying behind in the trenches (vide para 4 Operation Order No.20).
Rations for this party for July 30th will be provided by the S.A. Bde., and after that date by the 173rd Bde., with whom they will travel to SIMENCOURT.
This party will be under the orders of 2/Lt W.H.Richardson for travelling.

(c) On the 27th rations for consumption on the 28th only will be drawn for the personnel proceeding by march route.
Rations for the 29th for this party will be dumped at Staging Camp, ABLAINZEVELLE.

(d) Rations for the 30th inst. will be delivered at SIMENCOURT Camp on the 29th.

9. Refilling point on the 30th inst will be at LARESSET in lines of the 511th H.T.Coy: A.S.C.
Water can be obtained at SIMENCOURT at Q.17.a.1.4., Q.16.d.45.95. and Q.11.d.
E.F. Canteen at AVESNES-LES-COMTE.
There is a large Cinema Theatre at BERNEVILLE.

10. Sick will be collected from New Brigade Area by Horse Ambulances of the 2/3rd H.C.F.A. at WANQUETIN.

BY ORDER

HUGH W. PRIESTLEM
Capt & Adjutant.

Adjt

Copy 1

SECRET

2/8th BATTALION. LONDON REGIMENT. OPERATION ORDER No. 20.

Ref. Maps Sheet 57c. 1/40,000
Lens Sheet. 1/100,000. JULY 27th 1917.

1. The Battalion will be relieved by the 2nd S.A. Regt. on the night of the 28/29th, and will move by train and march route to Huts at SIMENCOURT breaking the journey at NEUVILLE Camp, P.22.c.2.5.

2. The order of the relief will be as follows:-

H.Q.	S.A. Regt.	will	relieve	H.Q.	P.O.R.	
A. Co.	"	"	"	"	C. Co.	"
D. Co.	"	"	"	"	A. Co.	"
B. Co.	"	"	"	"	B. Co.	"
C. Co.	"	"	"	"	D. Co.	"

3. One guide per platoon and one guide per Co. H.Q. will report to the Adjutant at Bn.H.Q. at 9.30.pm. July 28th to guide up incoming units. Each guide to have written instructions as to whom he has to guide up.

4. The following Officers will be left behind in the line 24 hours after relief:-

2/Lt G.W. CHANCELLOR A. Co.
2/Lt R.D. ROBINSON B. Co.
2/Lt W.H. RICHARDSON C. Co.

In addition A, B, & C Coys. will each leave behind 1 N.C.O. per platoon and 1 O.R. per Lewis Gun Team. Arrangements for their rations and their rejoining the Battalion will be found in para 8 b of Administrative Instructions, attached.

5. The Camp vacated by the 2nd S.A. Regt. at NEUVILLE will be taken over and the Battalion will proceed there by the 4 trains of the Light Railway which will bring the 2nd S.A. Regt to Point Q.9.d.2.6.

6. 2/Lt T.M. MacBeth will act as entraining Officer and will be at the Light Railway Terminus, point Q.9.d.2.6. from 9.30.pm onwards.
Headquarters and all platoons on being relieved will report to this Officer who will issue all necessary instructions with regard to entraining. On arrival at NEUVILLE the Battalion will form ~~ak~~ up by companies and will be taken to their lines by guides to be provided by 2/Lt MUMFORD.

7. All Officers' kits, mess baskets, Orderly Room Stores, M.O. Stores and anything that cannot be carried on the person will be taken back to Details Camp by Transport tonight, July 27th and must be dumped at Bn.H.Q. by 9.30.pm. 1 batman per company and 1 for H.Q. may proceed with the Transport to the Detail Camp inorder to ensure that Officers Smal kit, etc is put into their valises.

8. The usual receipts for Trench Stores handed over will be forwarded to Bn.H.Q.
All maps, intelligence reports, and Defence schemes will be handed over.
The work policy and details of work in progress will be carefully passed on.

9. Reliefs will be reported complete to Bn.H.Q. by wiring/ the code word "GIN"
Coy. Officers will also report to Bn.H.Q. personally.

10. The Battn., less marching portion of the Transport having

concentrated/

10. concentrated at NEUVILLE will move to BAPAUME by bus and road and will entrain from there to BEAUMETZ for SIMENCOURT in accordance with Administrative Instructions.

11. The marching portion of the Transport Section referred to above will move to SIMENCOURT by road on July 28/29th and will be under the orders of Lt T.A. Purkis.

12. Acknowledge.

[signature]
Capt & Adjutant.

Copies to:-

No. 1 War Diary.
2. C.O.
3. Adjutant.
4. A. Co.
5. B. Co.
6. C. Co.
7. D. Co.
8 H.Q.
9. T.O.
10. Q.M.
11. O.C. 2nd S.A. Regt.
12. M.O.
13. 2/Lt Mumford.

Army Form C. 2118.

Instructions regarding War Diaries and Intelligence Summaries are contained in F. S. Regs., Part II. and the Staff Manual respectively. Title pages will be prepared in manuscript.

WAR DIARY
or
INTELLIGENCE SUMMARY.
(Erase heading not required.)

2/8 London Rgt

2nd BATTALION. POST OFFICE RIFLES

1st August - 31st August 1917.

Vol 8

Place	Date	Hour	Summary of Events and Information	Remarks and references to Appendices
SIMENCOURT	Aug 1		2/Lt F. J. Edmonds rejoined from Hospital. JMM	
do	2		2/Lt F. J. Edmonds went on leave. JMM	
do	3		2/Lt C. A. Montgomery rejoined from leave. JMM	
do	4		2/Lt D. W. Lamb (London Scottish) joined for duty JMM	
do	5		2/Lt E. H. Edge, 2/Lieut J. Hitch joined for duty. JMM	
do	7		Lieutenant W. K. Ewen rejoined from duty with V Corps Gas office. 2/Lieut A. F. W. Blande JMM	
do			rejoins from III Army Infantry Course JMM	
do	8		2/Lieut W. H. Richardson. M.C. proceeded on leave. 6 Other ranks joined as reinforcements JMM	
do	10		Captain & Adjutant H.W. Priestley admitted to Hospital. 2/Lt C. A. Montgomery assumed the duties JMM	
do			of Adjutant. 35 Other ranks joined as reinforcements JMM	
do	12		Lieutenant W. K. Ewen admitted to Hospital. 2/Lieut J. P. R. Scrivener proceeded on L. Gun JMM	
do			Course XVII corps school. JMM	
do	13		2 Other ranks joined as reinforcements JMM	
do	14		2/Lieut F. J. Edmonds rejoin from leave. JMM	
do	16		Major C. B. Benson D.S.O. joins the battalion in the Field as Second in command JMM	
do	17		Major H. J. McClintock rejoins battalion for duty. 2/Lt A. F. W. Blande proceeded on leave. JMM	

T2134. Wt. W708—776. 500000. 4/15. Sir J. C. & S.

Instructions regarding War Diaries and Intelligence Summaries are contained in F. S. Regs., Part II. and the Staff Manual respectively. Title pages will be prepared in manuscript.

WAR DIARY
or
~~INTELLIGENCE~~ SUMMARY.
(Erase heading not required.)

Army Form C. 2118.

Place	Date	Hour	Summary of Events and Information	Remarks and references to Appendices
SIMENCOURT	Aug 19.		2/Lieut. C.A. Montgomery proceeded as an Instructor to 3rd Army Snipers School and relinquished	
do	"		duties of Adjutant. 2/Lt J.J. Mumford assumed the duties of Adjutant.	
do	" 20		27 Other ranks joined as reinforcements	
	" 21		Major H.J. McClintock and 5 Other ranks proceeded as advance party to new area.	
	" 23		A/Captain C. Kelly proceeded on leave.	
do	24	5 pm	The Battalion less C. Company left SIMENCOURT to proceed to new area. Entraining point ARRAS. The Battalion	
GODEWAERSVELDT	25		less C. Company, left by 9.54 pm train from ARRAS and detrained at GODEWAERSVELDE at 5.55 am	
			C. Company under Major P.E.M. Ash left SIMENCOURT at 4.45 am 25/8/17 proceeded by route	
			march to ARRAS and entrained, leaving ARRAS at 9.54 am detrained at GODEWAERSVELDE.	
	25		The Battalion left GODEWAERSVELDE to proceed by route march to camp at POPERINGHE. (A.22.d.7.7.) Sheet 28.	
			1st party arriving at 11.30 am 2nd party under Major Ash at 11.40 pm.	
BROWN CAMP (A22 d.7.7)	26		Major P.E.M. Ash, A/Captain A.D. Heaton. 2/Lt J.W. Sloan, 2/Lt R.B. Robinson. 2/Lt H. Booth	
			2/Lieut E.E.L. Teirsley. 2/Lt J.M.M. MacBeth. 2/Lt C.S. Armstrong proceeded on 3 days course	
			at XVIII Corps School.	
	21		2/Lieut H. Moss proceeded to attend XVIII Corps Infantry School.	
	21		Lt Col A.D. DERVICHE-Jones and 2/Lt Mumford reconnoitred routes to Brigade sector	

T2134. Wt. W708—776. 500000. 4/15. Sir J. C. & S.

Instructions regarding War Diaries and Intelligence Summaries are contained in F. S. Regs., Part II. and the Staff Manual respectively. Title pages will be prepared in manuscript.

WAR DIARY
or
~~INTELLIGENCE SUMMARY.~~
(Erase heading not required.)

Army Form C. 2118.

Place	Date	Hour	Summary of Events and Information	Remarks and references to Appendices
BROWN Camp (A22 d 77)	August 27		Major C.B. Benson DSO 2/Lt Chancellor, 2/Lt Hitch, 2/Lt Richardson MC and 2/Lt Watson reconnoitred Brigade forward area. Hon Lt and QM J. Gill went to hospital (SICK) today.	[initials]
	28		Major C.B. Benson DSO. 2/Lt Chancellor 2/Lt Richardson MC. Lt Shapley and Captn Massey-Miles RAMC reconnoitred Brigade forward area taking with them 12. O.R.	[initials]
			The Battalion moved today from BROWN CAMP (A22.d.77) to DAMBRE CAMP (B.27. a) by march route	[initials]
			SURPLUS BATTLE personnel 2/Lt Lamb and 116 O.R. proceeded by bus to DIVISIONAL DEPOT at HOUTKERQUE	[initials]
	30		Battalion moved from DAMBRE Camp. (B.27 a) to REIGERSBURG Camp (H 6 a & 8) by march route	[initials]
			2/Lt Blande rejoined from leave and was sent to join surplus battle personnel at HOUTKERQUE.	[initials]
	31		2/Lt Robinson, 2/Lt Hitch and 1. O.R. reconnoitred Brigade forward area today.	[initials]

[signature] Lt & Adjt.
7/8 Bn London Regt

[signature]
Lt. Col
Commanding 7/8 Battn London Regt.

T2134. Wt. W708—776. 500000. 4/15. Sir J. C. & S.

Instructions regarding War Diaries and Intelligence Summaries are contained in F. S. Regs., Part II. and the Staff Manual respectively. Title pages will be prepared in manuscript.

WAR DIARY
or
~~INTELLIGENCE~~ SUMMARY.
(Erase heading not required.)

174/58

Army Form C. 2118.

2/8th Bn The London Regt.
Post Office Rifles
1st Sept — 30th Sept.

Vol 9

Place	Date	Hour	Summary of Events and Information	Remarks and references to Appendices
	1917 Sept.			
REIGERSBERG	3		2/Lt E.E.L. TINSLEY evacuated sick to hospital. R.Y.Y.	
IN THE LINE	5/6		The Battalion relieved 2/6th Bn in the line, left Brigade Sector. 2/Lt T.M.M. MACBETH killed during relief. R.Y.Y.	APPENDIX I
	7		2/Lt J.P.B. SCRIVENER wounded. MAJOR C.B. BENSON. DSO. relieved Lt Col: DERVICHE-JONES MC. Front line shelled with mustard gas. R.Y.Y.	
	8		MAJOR P.C.M. ASH wounded during inter-company relief. 2/Lt H. BOOTH gassed during inter-company relief. R.Y.Y.	
	8/9		Battalion relieved by 2/5th Bn in the line & took over support Bn position in dug-outs on CANAL BANK from 2/6th Bn. R.Y.Y.	
CANAL BANK	9/10		Raid carried out by No 14 plat, D coy, led by 2/Lt O.H. WATSON, on enemy post at about C6d 65 95. Objects of raid — to kill boches, capture prisoners & secure identifications. Raiders were held up when 30 yds from post by wire entanglement — not observed in previous reconnaissance — they bombed post almost certainly killing garrison of 8. 2/Lt Watson was wounded early in the operation, but the raiders carried on & showed how complete their training had been. R.Y.Y.	APPENDIX II

T2134. Wt. W708—776. 500000. 4/15. Sir J. C. & S.

Instructions regarding War Diaries and Intelligence Summaries are contained in F. S. Regs., Part II. and the Staff Manual respectively. Title pages will be prepared in manuscript.

WAR DIARY
or
~~INTELLIGENCE SUMMARY.~~
(Erase heading not required.)

2/8 Bn The London Regt
Post Office Rifles
1st Sept — 30th Sept.

Army Form C. 2118.

Place	Date	Hour	Summary of Events and Information	Remarks and references to Appendices
CANAL BANK	Sept 10/11		L/Cpl McDougal R & 3 men (all of whom had taken part in raid on night of 9/10) went out to search the ground for their wounded comrades & 2nd Lt WATSON. They brought in 2 wounded men but could find no sign of their officer. On their return L/Cpl McDougal & TIMAN were wounded by a shell. R47.	
DAMBRE CAMP	11		Battalion relieved on Canal Bank by 2/2nd Bn & moved into DAMBRE CAMP. R47.	
	14.		Lt Col: DERVICHE-JONES attended a conference at Brigade H.Q to discuss future operations. R47.	
	15-18		The Bn in conjunction with the rest of the Bgde practiced the attack on a taped course. R47.	
REIGERSBURG CAMP.	18		The Bn moved to REIGERSBURG CAMP. R47	
	19		In the evening the Bn moved up to its position of assembly for the attack. R47.	Appendix 3 & 4
REIGERSBURG CAMP.	22/23		The Bn was relieved by 2/10th Bn & went to REIGERSBURG CAMP. R47.	
	24		The Bn moved to BRAKE CAMP at A 30 central. R47.	

T2134. Wt. W708—776. 500000. 4/15. Sir J. C. & S.

Instructions regarding War Diaries and Intelligence Summaries are contained in F. S. Regs., Part II. and the Staff Manual respectively. Title pages will be prepared in manuscript.

WAR DIARY
or
~~INTELLIGENCE SUMMARY.~~
(Erase heading not required.)

2/8 Bn The London Regt
Post Office Rifles
1st Sept — 30th Sept

Army Form C. 2118.

Place	Date	Hour	Summary of Events and Information	Remarks and references to Appendices
BRAKE CAMP.	26		Advance party left for LICQUES to prepare billets for Bn RYS.	
LANDRETHUN	27/28		Bn arrived in new area "C" & went into billets at LANDRETHUN & YEUSE. RYS.	
	29		Lt Col AD. DERVICHE JONES addressed the Bn for the first time after the attack. Brig Gen PEEL arrived with his staff & went away again.	RYS.

RY Ingilles ?
I.O. & asst. adj.

A.D. Derviche-Jones
Lt Col.
Commanding 2/8th Bn The London Regt.

T2134. Wt. W708—776. 500000. 4/15. Sir J. C. & S.

1724/58

Instructions regarding War Diaries and Intelligence Summaries are contained in F. S. Regs., Part II. and the Staff Manual respectively. Title pages will be prepared in manuscript.

WAR DIARY
or
~~INTELLIGENCE SUMMARY.~~
(Erase heading not required.)

Army Form C. 2118.

2/8 Bn The City of London Regt.
Sept 1st — Sept 30th

Place	Date	Hour	Summary of Events and Information	Remarks and references to Appendices
	14.		2/Lt J Mc I Brown joined divisional depot Bn.	
	16.		2/Lt R J F Carter 22 London Regt (Queens) joined Bn for duty.	
			2/Lt W J Ward 22 London Regt (Queens) joined Bn for duty.	
	17		Capt G E Gumming rejoined from course.	
	23		Major C B Benson DSO assumes command of the 2/6 Bn London Regt.	
	25		Lt Bostock J.A. 2/2 London Yeomanry joined the Bn in the field.	
			Capt E.B. Barnett joined the Bn for duty in the field.	
			2/Lt E.C.T. Finch "	
			" R. McAlister "	
			" E.F. Wilkinson. "	
			" H. Peacock "	
			" H. Moss rejoined Bn from Course.	
			" R.G. Barnes rejoined Bn " hospital.	

T2134. Wt. W708—776. 500000. 4/15. Sir J. C. & S.

6. TOOLS
No tools will be taken up.
A. Company will take over 7 picks & 30 shovels already in their posts
C. Company will take over 13 picks & 30 shovels already in their posts.
D. Company can draw tools when required from dump in the BUND

BUND dump has 14 picks & 151 shovels.

B. Company, will take over 20 picks & 46 shovels at their position.

7. BATTALION DUMP
Battalion forward magazine at HIBOU.

8. WATER
Support & Reserve companies will send parties to exchange petrol cans (empties for full) after dark at water dump on ADMIRALS Rd.

9. GRENADES
The 2/6th Bn. will hand over grenades to companies.

10. MOVEMENT
Great care must be taken in approaching all forward posts.
No movement in or round ~~in~~ these posts by day.

11. LIGHTS
Great care must be taken to screen ALL lights

12. SENTRIES
The R.S.M. will post a sentry at H.Q. to give warning in case of gas, enemy air-craft, and to keep down all movement round ALBERTA by day

13. SANITATION.
Proper attention must be paid to sanitation. Burial parties must be sent out from Forward & Support companies each night.

14. INTER-COMPANY RELIEFS on 7th ~~inst~~/8th inst.
1 platoon of C. Company will remain at HIBOU when inter-comy relief takes place and will be attached and under the orders of O.C. B. Company.
Co. Commanders will make the necessary arrangements.
Companies will not actually commence relief until midnight.
Relief to be complete by 3.am and reported to Bn.H.Q. by code word "GIN"
Other details have been issued separately.

15. RUNNERS.
While in the line a system of runners will be arranged by Lt Shapley.

16. The 2/7th Bn. London Regt. will take over accommodation vacated by this Battalion tonight.
Company Commanders will see that the Camp is left clean.

[signature]

Lieut & Adjutant,

APPENDIX II

SECRET. **2/8th Bn., The London Regiment.** Copy No: 3

SPECIAL O. O.

Ref: Sheet POELCAPELLE
1.10,000

1. On the night 9th/10th September a raid will be made on enemy posts situate about C.6.d.65.95 by a raiding party of 32 O.R. under 2/Lieut. O.H.WATSON.

2. Object of raid:-
   (a) To kill Boches.
   (b) To take prisoners.
   (c) To secure identifications and enemy maps and documents.

3. Plan of attack:-
   (a) The raiding party will be divided into two groups:-
   i. Covering party consisting of Platoon H.Q. and 10 O.R.
   ii. Attacking party
   (b) The raiding party will take up a position along the hedge running N.W. from C.6.d.55.78. at 15 minutes before Zero.
   (c) The covering party will be disposed in two posts:-
   i. Platoon H.Q., S.B.Squad and 5 O.R. at about C.6.d.40.90.
   ii. 5 O.R. at about C.6.d.45.80. with about 50 yards between the posts, and will remain at their posts until the attacking party has withdrawn. The object of the covering party is to engage the enemy posts at C.6.d.65.95. from the moment when enemy fire is opened from these posts until the attacking party is within rushing distance of the posts and also to cover the withdrawal of the attacking party.
   (d) At Zero the attacking party will work up the hedge running N.E. from C.6.d.55.78. and will attack the enemy posts from the flank.
   (e) The attacking party will withdraw at Zero plus 20, when a signal of two pairs of white Very Lights will be fired from platoon H.Q. and reassemble at the place of rendezvous.

4. Artillery.
   Artillery will co-operate in the following manner:-
   (a) Short crashes along the enemy front including the hedge running in N.W. from C.6.d.55. 78. and enemy posts at C.6.d.65.95. from 8.pm. to 8.55. pm.
   (b) From Zero to Zero plus 30 Hows. will engage enemy strong points at C.6.d.89.57. and C.6.d. 80. 29. and 18 pounders will barrage from C.6.d.80.30. to C.6.d.8070.
   The barrage will not be intense but be of the nature of neutralising fire.

5. Place of rendezvous.
   Left company post just behind the N. apex of the TRIANGLE.

Contd.

B.S.O./30/9.
O.C. Unbind

9.9.17.

Reference para. 5 of 174th Inf. Bde Order No. 44.

I A direct line from Brigade Headquarters to the BUND will be provided, and reserved for use of UNBIND.
Signal Officer UNDER will provide operator and D3 at the BUND, and will also make certain connections as detailed in para. 2 and 3 below.
The operator will have head receivers to ear from Zero – 15 mins to Zero + 1 hour.
He will call direct to BJ; no exchanges will be intermediate. Line will be OK'ed every 5 minutes.

2 At 8.45 p.m. Cpl. Adams will test to BJ and to RK on the ordinary lines (bury to M.T., light armoured twin MT to RK) and put these through off the exchange, leaving a D3 in loop for linesmans purposes. He will be responsible

for sending out on the ditch if he hears no OK or message for 10 minutes.
Sigs UNDER will put through this same line to the BUND, putting it through direct and not via an exchange. He will have no instrument tied in.

3 Cpl. Adams will arrange communication from MT to RK on one pair of the quad cable, which he will put on his exchange and test the RK end of this will be manned by Sigs UNDER at 8.30 with a D3.

The second line from MT to Divn. will be used by Cpl. Adams in putting cables from RK through to Brigade, via Divnl. exchange.

4 Cpl. Adams will wire code word XERXES to Sigs BJ when the changes made in 3 and 4 are complete and OK.

5 The visual between WG and the BUND will be operated by Sigs. UNDER, but reserved for use of UNBIND from Zero – 15 to Zero + 1 hour. After that operation messages from UNBIND have priority over the visual for the remainder of the night.

6. Two message dogs will be at Maison du Hibou by Zero – 30 minutes under care of a runner from Brigade.

7. Acknowledge.

5.0 pm

D. C. Henry Lt

Signal Officer,

174th Infantry Brigade.

Copies to

O.C UNBIND
SIGS UNBIND
SIGS UNDER
CPL ADAMS

Ref: Trench Map
1.5000

PATROLS.

1. The Battalion will probably take over and hold the Brigade front on the night of the 5th/6th September.

2. It is of the UTMOST IMPORTANCE that the Brigade front should be effectively patrolled EVERY night for the following purposes:-
   i. Information as to:-
      (a) The state of the ground up to the enemy lines.
      (b) What the enemy is doing.
      (c) What places he is holding and in what strength.
      (d) Presence or absence and condition of wire - MEBUSES and other Strong points in or in front or behind his lines.

   ii. To harass and kill the enemy and to prevent him wiring or improving his position.

   iii. To take prisoners.

   iv. and generally to get supreme control of NO MAN'S LAND

3. With these objects in view.
   (a) each Company holding the front lines will send out <u>two patrols each night</u> at different parts of the line.
   (b) Each patrol must have a definite task assigned to it and must be in charge of an <u>officer</u> or <u>reliable N.C.O.</u> (at least one patrol from each front company per night must be an <u>officer's</u> patrol.)
   (c) If enemy is seen either working or walking about, IMMEDIATE ACTION must be taken either by rifle fire from patrol or by sending back to the post and getting L.G. fire on the enemy. ON NO ACCOUNT is the enemy to be allowed <u>to work unmolested</u>. If a patrol returns to get L.G. fire on to the enemy this does not finish the patrol's job; it must go out again until it has completed the task assigned to it.

4. For patrol purposes areas assigned to companies are as follows:-
   (a) <u>Right front companie</u>
      i. <u>right boundary</u>; line drawn from N.W. corner of SPRINGFIELD to road junction D.7.a.10.90.
      ii. <u>left boundary</u>; line from CROSS Roads C.6.d.20.29. to first <u>E</u>. in HUBNER TRENCH.

   (b) <u>LEFT front Company</u>.
      from the first <u>E</u> in HUBNER TRENCH to line drawn from Cross Roads C.6.b.10.50. to Road junction C.6.b.75.25.

   (c) D. Company will also nightly send a patrol for a special purpose to reconnoitre enemy strong point at C.6.b.70.20.

5. Owing to difficulties of communication which can only take place at night Company Commanders will arrange all details of their patrols without further order from Bn. H.Q. and will arrange to warn troops on flanks.

6. All titles must be removed and papers left behind by patrol parties.

7. On night of inter company relief, patrols will be sent out as usual by the Company holding the front line and waiting to be relieved.

P.T.O.

6. All patrol reports must be tabulated on a special form (a pro forma is attached) and reach Bn. H.Q. in time for the Company runner to return before dawn.
No movement whatever is allowed above ground during the day.

REPORT on MINOR ENTERPRISE by 2/8th Bn. London Regt.
Carried out on night 9/10th Sept. 1917.

---

1. The objective of the raid was a fortified shell hole at C.6.d.65.95 by a party of 32 O.R. under 2/Lt O.H. WATSON.

2. Previous reconnaissance had been made by patrols under 2/Lt Watson, Cpl MacDougall and 10 O.R.s on four succeeding nights.

3. At 8.30.pm the raiding party arrived at the RENDEZVOUS just behind the N Apex of the TRIANGLE (C.6.c.70.50.) without ~~xxx~~ incident and remained there until 9.pm. *Zero was fixed for 9.30. pm*

4. At 9.pm the party moved from the Rendezvous viâ the POELCAPELLE - ST JULIEN Road to C.6 central, thence along the hedge running first S.E. then N.E. and then again S.E. taking up the position previously arranged along the hedge running N.W. from C.6.d.55.78. at about 9.15.pm.
On reaching the derelict tank on the POELCAPELLE - ST JULIEN Road at C.6.c.85.70 the party had to take cover from some crashes of our shrapnel falling between this road and HUBNER Trench. Some shrapnel fell very short, from 15 to 30 yards from the road, wounding one man of the raiding party (time 9.3.pm)

5. At 9.15.pm the party divided into three groups as arranged:-
   (a) No 1 group (covering party) Platoon H.Q., S.B. Squad and 5 O.R.s remaining at about C.6.d.40.98.
   (b) No 2 group (covering party) 5 O.R.s at about C.6.d.50.88
   (c) No 3 group (attacking party) Cpl MacDougall and 17 O.R. lying close to the S.E. corner of the hedge at about C.6.d.55.78.

6. At 9.20.pm the enemy sent up two red lights followed quickly by two green lights from the shell hole at C.6.d.65.95 and immediately started M.G. and rifle fire on the hedge where the raiding party had taken up position. It is belived that the movement of the party along this hedge had been noticed by the enemy.

7. It had been previously arranged that, if the enemy should send up a S.O.S. or detect the party <u>before</u> Zero, the attacking party should start off at once, without waiting for Zero. The attacking party accordingly started as soon as the enemy fire opened, at 9.22.pm and proceeded about 30 yards N.E. along the hedge where the ground ~~was~~ *became* impassable owing to water and thence in open order almost due N to the objective.

8. (a) Report of attacking party:-
   (i) The open ground between the hedge and the objective was much cut up but fairly dry and no difficulty was encountered until about 30 feet from the objective, when a belt of new wire 15 feet thick was encountered. This wire was not visible from the hedge and had not been discovered by reconnaissance.

ii/

(ii) Enemy was firing with light M.G. from objective and threw a number of egg bombs at the attacking party, wounded two.

Mills bombs were lobbed easily into shell hole, which contained eight Boche, and must have been effective, as all fire both of M.G., rifle and of bombs ceased from the shell hole. Owing to the noise it was impossible to distinguish cries, but all the bombs thrown hit the mark and burst.

(iii) Careful investigation was then made of the shell hole and the immediate surroundings, and it was observed that this shell hole was connected by a trench in the rear with a number of small shell holes and ultimately with a MEBUS (concrete) showing 3' 6" above the ground and having two frontal openings (approximate position of MEBUS C.6.d.73.~~95~~ 93) This MEBUS is about 40 yards from the big shell hole.

Rifle fire was then directed on the frontal openings of the MEBUS, from which a considerable amount of M.G. fire had been directed, until the previously arranged signal for withdrawal (4 white Very Lights) was sent up from Plateon H.Q. at about 9.40. pm.

(iv) The attacking party then withdrew to the hedge without further casualty, searched the hedge for wounded of the covering party, ~~and~~ got in five wounded and then withdrew to the Rendezvous, where they were joined by the survivors (unwounded) of the covering party.

(v) Casualties to attacking party:-
Two wounded by Egg bombs.
One by M.G. (two others were shot by M.G. through the steel helmet without being hurt).

(b) Report of covering party:-

(i) Almost immediately after the Boche red and green signals Our Artillery fired crashes along and in front of the hedge where the covering party was, killing two O.R.s. wounding 2/Lieut. O.H.Watson and 4. O.R. (time 9.25. pm.) A further Artillery crash occurred (wounding 2 more) but the time cannot be fixed; it would probably be just after 9.40.pm as L/Corpl Hickman fired the Signal to return at 9.40.pm and was wounded (and missing) immediately afterwards.

(ii) 2/Lieut. O.H.WATSON was wounded at about 9.25. pm., as he was moving from Plateon H.Q. along the hedge to see that the attacking party was ready. He had 2 S.B.s. and an orderly with him, all of whom were wounded.

31.

GENERAL REMARKS

(a) ARTILLERY

i. Hostile The raiding party were never troubled by hostile artillery. Enemy barraged HIBOU and the STEENBEEK seven minutes after the enemy red and green signal went up.

ii. Our Own Artillery

The neutralising fire on HUBNER and MEBUSES was effective: at any rate no rifle or M.G. fire came on the party from that direction.

There were, what appears to be, two serious errors:-

1. In the Time Table. Firstly the "crashes" did not cease between 9.pm and 9.30.pm, on the area - hedge and objective.
It was arranged that there should be no crashes N of C.6.d.80.56 between 9.pm & 9.30.pm.

2. In firing shorts:-
One of the party was wounded on the ST JULIEN road and it is reported that some men of the 2/5th in the outpost in front of the road were wounded.

(b) The leadership both of 2/Lt O.H. WATSON and Corporal MacDougall was excellent. It was unfortunate that the attack was held up by wire invisible to the reconnoitring parties, but enemy were undoubtedly put out of action and valuable information obtained of the enemy's defences. The whole raid went off as ~~organised~~ organised and planned up to the moment the unknown wire was encountered.
It is regretable that 2/Lt Watson is wounded and missing. I desire to mention particularly this officer and Corporal MacDougall, both of whom spent 4 nights in reconnaissance and were indefatigable in the preparation for and carrying out of the enterprise.

(c) Total casualties

	Officers.	O.R.s	Cause
Killed.		3	Our Artillery
Wounded	1 (missing)	7	" "
"		2	Boche bombs
"		1	Boche M.G.

(d) Enemy defences

i. Close to the fortified shell hole is a small shell hole used for observation and listening.

ii. The big shell hole is protected by a swamp 15feet wide on the northerly side and around two sides by a belt of wire (new) 15 feet thick connecting up with the front line wire.

iii. At the rear of the shell hole is a narrow trench connecting up with 3 small shell holes and eventually with a concrete MEBUS, standing 2' 6" above ground and having two frontal openings. This MEBUS is about 40 yards to rear of the shell hole. (sketch attached).

10.9.17

Lt-Colonel.
COMMANDING 2/8th Battn. London Regiment

SECRET.

2/8th Bn., The London Regiment.
Special O. O.

6. DRESS.
(a) Drill Order with Box Respirators at alert.
(b) Rifles and fixed bayonets.
(c) Helmets covered with cap comforters.
(d) Jack knives.
(e) Covering party one round in breech.
1 clip in magazine.
5 spare clips in pockets.
Eight Hales grenades will be carried and only be used by special rifle grenadiers selected by 2/Lieut. O.H.WATSON.
(f) Attacking party. one round in breech.
1 clip in magazine.
2 spare clips in pockets.
2 bombs apiece will be carried by two special bombers to be seåected by 2/Lieut. O.H.WATSON.

7. Stretcher Bearer Squad will go with Platoon H.Q.

8. Raiding party will carry no papers, letters, pay-books or identification marks (except their discs)

9. Prisoners will be disarmed and sent back with as small an escort as possible to Platoon H.Q.

10. Papers should be taken and buttons and shoulder straps removed by knife from uniforms of any Boche killed.

SECRET (3) 2/8th BATTALION. LONDON REGIMENT. Copy No. 12

OPERATION ORDER No.6

Reference. Sheet 28 N.W. 1/20,000
POELCAPELLE Edn. 2
1/10,000

18.9.17.

---

1. The attack on the enemy is to be renewed on Z day, a date which has been communicated verbally to Company Commanders at an hour to be notified later.

2. (a) The 55th Division will be attacking on the right of the 58th Division and the 51st Division on the left.

(b) The attack on the 58th Division front will be carried out by the 174th Infantry Brigade.

(c) The 173rd Brigade will co-operate with an attack on WINNIPAG FARM (4th London Regiment)

3. The 174th Brigade will attack on a one battalion front.

1st Phase. The 8th London Regiment will capture, mop up and consolidate up to and along the dotted Blue line, shown on an objective map already in the possession of Company Commanders.

2nd Phase. The BROWN LINE by the 5th Battn. passing through the 8th Battn.

3rd Phase. The BLUE LINE by the 6th Battn. passing through the 8th and 5th battalions.

4. ASSEMBLY :- on Y - Z night -
The 8th Battn. will assemble along a taped line E of the KEERSELARE - SPRINGFIELD Road except on the right where the tape will cut this road at C.12.b.30.80., and the right will rest on a spot 30 yards W of SPRINGFIELD Mebus.

(a) Taping party
A taping party consisting of CAPT HEATON, two officers already detailed and two O.R.s from each company will march from REIGERSBURG Camp at 8.30.pm on Y - Z night and tape out the line of assembly.

(b) Guides
With the taping party will be a party of guides, one from each platoon, under 2/Lieut TREGELLES.
Each guide will carry a disc marked with the number of his platoon, which he will fix in the ground allotted to his platoon front.
Guides will assemble with Lt TREGELLES at 12.30.am at a spot just behind (i.e. W of) the N Apex of the Triangle (which will be H.Q. of O i/c Assembly) where they will meet platoons as they arrive; each guide will conduct his own platoon to his platoon position of assembly, having previously reconnoitred the route with the taping party.

(c) Taping party and guides will be under the command of Capt HEATON, who is O i/c Assembly and who will make all arrangements for and supervise the assembly of the battalion and will report at Bn.H.Q. as soon as the Battn. is all in position.

(d)

(d) The battalion must be in position by 3.am night Y - Z.

(e) Bn.H.Q. will parade, ready to start under Lt SHAPLEY at 7.30.pm. and proceed direct to HIBOU (C)

(f) The remainder of the Battalion will parade ready to start at 11.pm and will march by platoons at 200 yards distance in the following order:-

A. - C. - D, - B.

(g) COVERING PARTIES

i. Arrangements are being made for the 7th Battn. to provide covering parties for the taping of the line of Assembly.

ii. Each Company will find its own covering party for the assembly.

(h) The greatest attention must be paid to avoiding noise or confusion in the assembly. Discovery by the enemy would mean large casualties before the attack and materially prejudice the success of the operation. All men must be warned that they may have to put on box respirators in passing through certain areas and must be prepared to do so without confusion or delay.

5. DISPOSITIONS AND FORMATIONS

(a) The battalion will attack on a four company front.

(b) Each company will be formed up on a two platoon front.

(c) Company and platoon objectives have already been allotted

(d) Each company will have two sections (one of which should be a L.G. Section) attached to Company H.Q. as Company Commanders reserve. This reserve should not get involved in the initial fighting but be kept fresh for contingencies.

(e) One platoon of each company detailed to capture an area of the LANGEMARK line will be re-organised as soon as rear platoons have passed through them and will become battalion reserve.
These platoons must be rested as much as possible but may be used on the iniative of Commanders without waiting for orders from Bn.H.Q.

(f) Front platoons will advance with two sections extended and two sections in file:
rear platoons in line of half platoons.

6. PLAN OF ATTACK

This has already been explained to Commanders and is on the basis that every platoon has a definite area to attack, capture, mop up and consolidate. Companies will arrange for mutual co-operation in the capture of Enemy Strong points.

7./

7. Strong points:-

(a) by "A" Company at:-

i. MEBUS at extreme right boundary - a double block must be established here in DIMPLE TRENCH.

ii. At D.1.c.20.00. (MEBUS in Triangle)

iii. At D.1.c.30.00. (ruined farm buildings)

either No: ii oriii must be garrisoned by a platoon (with a L.G.)

(b) by C. Company at:- GENOA Farm.

(c) by B. Company one at each ~~at~~ group of 5 Mebuses.

(d) by D. Company:-

i. At HUBNER FARM

ii. At C.6.b.80.00.

these Strong points will provide frontal defence and defence on both flanks. Strong points b.c.d. ~~require~~ require each a garrison of one platoon.

(e) D. Company will also establish 2 posts at least along road from Hubner Farm to D.1.a.36.20.

8. M.G.s.

(a) Two guns will assemble with C. Coys. H.Q. and advance in rear of the Company to the Bulge where they will remain until the Triangle redoubts are captured, when they move up to MEBUS at D.1.c.20.00.

(b) Two guns will assemble with B. Coys. H.Q. and advance in rear of Company. The allotted positions of these guns are:-

i. MEBUS at D.1.c.30.55.

ii. HUBNER FARM.

Tanks.

9.(a) One Section of Tanks will cooperate with this battalion.

Objectives:-

i. Strong point C.6.d.80.00.

ii. MEBUSES D.7.a.00.85.

iii. MEBUSES in road Triangle about D.1.c.10.00.

Route:- Road from Triangle ~~Farm~~ Farm to D.7.a.05.95.

(b) All ranks are to be warned that they are on no account to wait for Tanks.

(c) If a tank gets ahead it is the duty of Infantry to push on and support it.

(d) No request by a Tank for assistance in the forming of a strong point in advance of the line or overcoming hostile resistance is to be refused or neglected.

10. Cantact Aeroplane.

(a) A. contact aeroplane will fly over the objectives at:-

i. Zero plus 1 hour.

ii. " " 2 hours and 30 minutes.

iii. " " 4 hours.

and at other times.

(b) Infantry in front lines will be ready to light red flares (in groups of 3) at these hours but will NOT do so unless called for by aeroplane sounding its FLAXON Horn or dropping white lights.

11. BARRAGE.

(a) The attack will be preceeded by an intense bombardment for 24 hours.

(b) A creeping barrage will be opened at Zero about 150 yards in front of the leading lines of assembly and will creep forward inlifts of 50 yards.

1st lift at Zero + 3
2nd lift at " + 5.
3rd " " " + 7.
4th " " " + 9.
5th " " " + 12.

and so on until dotted blue line is reached.

(c) A protector barrage on a line 150 yds in front of dotted blue line will stand until Zero + 1 hour and 25 minutes.

12. LIAISON.

(a) After assembly D. Company will get in touch with 9th Royal Scots on left.

(b) As soon as HUBNER Farm is captured O.C. D. Company will send forward the special LIAISON Section to Track and road junction S.E. of FRORA Cott. (D.1.a.66.20) The duty of this section is :-

i. To get in touch with 9th Royal Scots.

ii. To inform them what posts and strong points we hold on our left flank.

iii. To get information of Royal Scot posts ans send same back to O.C. D. Company.

iv. To hold the post at the cross roads jointly with the 9th Royal Scots Section until relieved.

(c) By A. Company at D.7.a.00.90. with 4th London Regiment.

13. H.Q.

(a) Bn. Mon du HIBOU. (c & d)

(b) A. Co. i. Assembly at N.W. corner of SPRINGFIELD.
ii. Moves forward to MEBUS C.12.b.95.80.

(c) C. Co. i. Assembly at C.6.d.25.10.
ii. Moves to C.6.d.80.20. (left MEBUS or Bulge)

(d) B. Co. i. Assembly at C.6.d.20.50.
ii. Moves to C.6.d.90.45. (Mebus)

(e) D. Co i. Assembly at C.6.d. 05.70.
ii. Moves to D.1.c.15.73. (one of 5 Mebuses)

each Company will carry a flag to mark Coy. H.Q

(f) Brigade H.Q. 5
6.pm. on Y day at C.17.c.1.8.

(f) contd.
Forward Station at i. HIBOU
ii. SPRINGFIELD.

14. TIME
Watches will be synchronised at Orderly Room at 6.pm on Y day.

15. Administrative Orders issued separately.

A D Derviche-Jones

Lt-Colonel.
Commanding 2/8th Battalion. London Regiment.

Issued 18.9.17

Copies to No. 1 Commanding Officer.
2 Major Benson, D.S.O.
3 Captain Heaton
4. Intelligence Officer
5. Signalling Officer
6. O.C. "A" Company.
7. O.C. "B" "
8. O.C. "C" "
9. O.C. "D" "
10. 174th Infantry Brigade
11. O.C. 9th Royal Scots.
12. Adjutant.
13. O.C. 2/5th London Regt.
14. O.C. 2/6th "
15. O.C. 2/7th "
16. O.C. 198 M.G. Co.
17. O.C. Tanks.
18. War Diary.
19. O.C. 2/4th London Regt.
20. Liaison Officer.

Headquarters,

174th Infantry Brigade.

2/8th BATTALION, LONDON REGIMENT

Report on OPERATIONS of 20th September 1917

ALBERTA Section (YPRES)

I have the honour to submit the following report of the Action of this battalion in the above operations :-

(1), ASSEMBLY

(a) i. The taping party consisting of Capt HEATON, 2/Lieut TREGELLES, 2/Lieut CHANCELLOR, 2/Lieut HITCH, and two N.C.O.s from each company and 16 platoon guides left REIGERSBURG Camp at 8.pm 19/20 September. The party was under the direct command of Capt. HEATON, who was responsible for the taping of the line of Assembly and for the Assembly of the battalion.

ii. H.Q. of the taping party was at the N Apex of TRIANGLE FARM.

iii. No difficulty was experienced in taping the line, which was completed within one hour after the party had reached their H.Q.

iv. Intermittent hostile M.G. fire caused one casualty to this party. There was also some heavy enemy shelling on the St JULIEN Road from time to time.

(b) i. The battalion left REIGERSBURG Camp at 10.pm, marching by platoons at 200 yards distance.

ii. Considerable delay was caused :-
Firstly by a M.G. Section in front which was heavily laden and could only proceed slowly.
Secondly by the rain which made the duck boards greasy.
Thirdly by gaps in the track caused by hostile shelling. In one place a derelict TANK lay right across the track and it was extremely difficult to get round it. Again, an ammunition train had pulled up across the track and all the troops had to climb over the trucks.

iii. The result of these delays caused the battalion to arrive 1½ hours late at the H.Q. Assembly.

iv/

iv. Platoons guides met the battalion and each platoon was guided to its position quickly.

v. Touch was found with the 2/4th on the right and with the 9th Royal Scots on the left.

vi. The whole battalion was in position by 3.45.am.

(c) There was considerable hostile shelling in the neighbourhood of the track during Assembly, especially by ADMIRAL'S Road, KITCHENER'S WOOD, ALBERTA and HIBOU but practically none along the line of Assembly.

(d) The taping and the assembly proceeded exactly as rehearsed during training and great credit is due to those responsible, especially to Capt. HEATON, for getting the battalion into position with only <u>one</u> casualty.

(e) <u>STRENGTH of Battalion at Zero</u>

	Officers.	O.R.s
"A" Company.	3	98
"B" "	3	94
"C" "	3	110
"D" "	3	99
H.Q.	5	32
	17	433

(2). <u>THE ATTACK.</u>

A. <u>Preliminary</u>

(a) <u>Dispositions</u>. The Battalion was formed up on a four company front, from Right to left A.C.B.D. and each company on a two platoon front.

(b) <u>Formations</u>. The advance was made with each front platoon having two sections extended to form a long continuous line of skirmishers covering the battalion front of 700 yards, the remaining sections of front platoons in file. Rear platoons in half platoons in file disposed according to the position of their objectives.

(c) <u>Reserves</u>. Attached to H.Q. of each company were two sections (one a L.G. Section) to act as Company Commanders reserve.

(d) <u>Plan of attack.</u> To each company was assigned a definite area, containing a known strong point of Resistance :-

To A. Company.	MARINE VIEW
To C. "	The Promenade and GENOA FARM.
To B. "	Two groups of ten "pill boxes"
To D. "	HUBNER FARM.

(e) Each platoon was given a definite area to attack, capture, mop up and consolidate.

(f) The flanks and direction of the advance had been well reconnoitred previous to the attack.

B. FROM ZERO

(a) At Zero 5.40.am the whole line of skirmishers advanced followed by the rest of the battalion in the formations and order arranged, close up behind the skirmishers in order to keep up with the barrage.

(b) Reports of each company from right to left are submitted :-

1. "A"Company. At Zero as our barrage came down, our line advanced and for the first 50 yards no opposition was encountered; at this point considerable M.G. and rifle fire was met with, and No. 4 platoon was wiped out with the exception of 5 men, 2/Lieut SLOAN being killed. The fire came from two directions GENOA and ARENA. The line continued to advance to within 30 yards of the enemy posts in front of the LANGEMARK line under heavy M.G. and rifle fire. At this point there was a check, but the enemy was engaged with Rifle Grenades and L.Gs, and while parties crept round the flanks of the enemy positions, where most of the enemy surrendered, the remainder, who continued to offer resistance being killed. On the extreme right, an enemy post of 12 men were encountered, who fled as soon as they saw our men getting round their right flank. From this point no further organised resistance was encountered and the company continued to advance, mopping up dug outs and pill boxes. DIMPLE Trench was entirely captured and the platoon detailed for MARINE VIEW had no difficulty in effecting its captures, despite M.G. fire from GENOA FARM.
All objectives were taken in about 45 minutes after Zero and consolidation at once put in hand. All the Officers of the company having become casualties Sergt. HARRIS took command, reorganised the company and selected posts for consolidation. Touch was maintained with the 2/4th throughout the advance and a party of the 2/4th who crossed our front was utilised to garrison a portion of DIMPLE Trench, thus enabling No. 2 Platoon to extend to its left and to mop up and hold the objective detailed to No. 4 platoon which had been almost wiped out before reaching its objective. Posts were established in front of DIMPLE Trench at MARINE VIEW.
A joint Company H.Q. with "C" Company was established at the left PILL BOX of the PROMENADE.
The enemy barraged MARINE VIEW and DIMPLE TRENCH at about 1½ hours after Zero and again at 6.pm on the 21st.
Soon after Zero four twin green lights were sent up from PILL BOX at MARINE VIEW.
During the attack the enemy discharged canisters of liquid fire on our right flank.
About 40 prisoners were sent back, and 2 M.G.s captured.

ii. C. Company

Our line advanced at Zero and encountered no opposition until about 100 yards from the

PROMENADE /

PROMENADE, when it came under heavy M.G. and rifle fire and stick bombs thrown from shell holes: a certain number of liquid fire bombs were also thrown.
The advance was temporarily checked while the enemy posts were engaged with L.G.s and rifle grenades; at the same time parties were sent round the flanks of the enemy positions, which were rushed.
At the left PILL BOX of the PROMENADE, as soon as the flanking parties got into position some 50 prisoners were taken, surrendering as soon as they were outflanked.
The company was then reorganised by 2/Lt RICHARDSON, who had been previously wounded and the advance continued to GENOA FARM which was captured with slight resistance owing to flanking fire brought on to it by a flank company. Beyond GENOA the advance continued close up to the barrage and covering fire given to the 2/8th as they came up.
After the 2/8th had passed through the advanced line returned to GENOA and made posts there.
In the meantime posts were constructed in the PROMENADE.
When all the officers of the company became casualties Sergt FRANCIS assumed command, selected posts and directed consolidation.
About 1½ hours after Zero enemy barrage came down on GENOA, The PROMENADE and HUBNER Trench, where it remained ½ hour lifting to HIBOU and the TRIANGLE FARM, and again at 6.pm on the 21st lasting until 6.15.pm to cover a counter attack.
An interesting ~~FRENCH~~ MAP is attached showing the enemy dispositions in the PROMENADE. The original (sent herewith) was picked up on a table in HUBNER FARM (the enemy Battalion Commander's H.Q.)
This MAP is marked "A"

iii. B. Company

At Zero an advance was made up to within 30 yards of the barrage. The ground was very broken and the advance was slow but we were able to keep within 30 yards of the barrage right up to the final objectives.
No difficulty was experienced in crossing the wire in front of HUBNER Trench. This trench was captured without difficulty; it was found to be a mass of shell holes, some half covered over with timber and camouflage. In some cases these shell holes were garrisoned by one or two men with light M.G.s. In every instance they were dealt with either by shooting the gunners or rushing them with the bayonet.
It was found, however, necessary to get up to 10 yards of the barrage in order to rush these posts. In two instances a Sergeant rushed through our barrage and bayonetted the gunners who were causing casualties with their fire. One particular instance is worthy of mention when this Sergeant (Sergt Knight) rushed through our barrage to a post of 12 of the enemy, shot one bayonetted two and scattered the rest, capturing the M.G., all unaided.
Most of the M.G. fire came from the flanks and from a way behind but the advance never wavered and was continued in its original formations.
A few light shells fell on our taped line about 20 minutes after Zero.
As the platoons detailed for the two groups of PILL BOXES advanced through the front platoons, they came under enfilade fire from GENOA FARM; this fire was slight and not maintained.

Observing /

Observing that the company on the right was having some difficulty with GENOA FARM, we detached a L.G. and a few men to give them covering fire.

At this point some of the 7th Argyll & Sutherland Highlanders began to push across our left flank. We had to conform and our right platoon dropped back slightly until in line with No. 6 platoon.

These platoons were in charge of Sergeant KNIGHT, who led them on to the capture of the right group of PILL BOXES.

We then attacked the left group reinforced by the reserves and company H.Q. Here we captured two Officers and some M.G.s.

At this time the attack on HUBNER FARM on the left front was developing and a L.G. was detached to give covering fire on the enemy in shell holes in rear of the farm.

All objectives were taken by 6.10.am and consolidation started.

At 7.15.am a heavy hostile bombardment was started on HUBNER Trench and the PILL Boxes; by this time the men were well dug in in front and on the flanks of the PILL Boxes and we had no casualties from shell fire.

Enemy Aeroplanes also flew low over our position.

At 6.pm another hostile barrage was put on our positions and enemy were observed forming up for a counter attack, which did not developed owing to our barrage.

At 5.30.pm on the 21st the enemy again bombarded us, but their counter attack did not develope owing to our barrage.

This company captured 2 officers and 20 O.R.s also the following guns:-

<u>1 Heavy M.G.</u> in working order, captured at D.1.c.15.60 and handed over to 198th M.G. Company and used by them in HUBNER FARM.

<u>1 Light M.G.</u> taken in shell hole at C.6.d.70.60. Handed over to 198th M.G. Company.

<u>1 Light M.G.</u> taken at C.6.d.80.45, and later destroyed by shell fire.

<u>2 Light M.G.s</u> taken at D.1.c.20.40., which were found to be damaged by our barrage and left behind with the 2/10th on relief.

iv. <u>D. Company</u>

The line advanced smartly at Zero and the front troops kept up to 20 yards from the barrage, the shells bursting well behind their heads. Some casualties, a few, occurred from our barrage and some from M.G. fire, reducing the leading platoons, which were weak, to about half their strength.

2/Lieut. ARMSTRONG with the 5 men left in his platoon attacked point 20 which was a chain of fortified shell holes and captured it, killing 10 with bayonet and revolver, and taking 4 prisoners.

The 9th Royal Scots appeared to be crossing this front and this post was handed over to them, so as to release 2/Lieut. ARMSTRONG and his 5 men and another 3 whom he collected to mop up the section of HUBNER Trench on the right and to advance and assist in the Mopping up of HUBNER FARM.

No. 14 platoon on the right received severe attention from FLORA COTT and took their objective with only 6 O.R.s.

They consolidated in a large shell hole and were subsequently used as company reserve.

Strenuous /

Strenuous resistance was met round HUBNER FARM from the enemy who were not only in the farm but in shell holes in the rear and on the flanks.
No. 15 platoon was detailed to capture this farm, this platoon arrived in the neighbourhood with one L.G. Corporal (with his gun) and 4 men, who immediately took up a position and engaged the entrances to the farm. In the meantime "B" Company on the right had detached a L.G. to engage the parties of enemy in shell holes and a party of 9th Royal Scots (4 in numbers) moved to the left flank and fired while 5 men of the 2/5th L.R.B. crept up to the left flank and got in rear of the farm. The farm was then rushed and the defence cracked up, between 70 & 100 prisoners throwing down their arms and surrending. They were unwounded men; in addition a great number were killed and there were 30 wounded enemy in the farm and 2 medical officers and 8 stretcher bearers.
No. 16 platoon in the meantime advanced slightly in rear and to the left of No. 15 as had been arranged and took their objectives without difficulty.
As soon as the attack had succeeded, 2/Lieut ARMSTRONG and his men were moved up to relieve the 9th Royal Scots and men of the 2/5th, who had assisted in the capture of the farm and who rejoined their units.
3 Heavy M.G.s were captured in this farm.
Consolidation was put in hand at once and a strong line of posts made from D.1.a.66.30 just behind the road leading from there to HUBNER FARM and in front of the farm.
Enemy barraged behind our front posts at 5.30.pm and fired a few intermittent shells before that.
Again on the 21st in the afternoon there was a heavy hostile bombardment on our posts and some lumps were taken off HUBNER FARM - we had no casualties in our posts.

v. The above are the reports from my companies. They furnish a fine story of dash, initiative and able dispositions and leadership.
Credit must be given to the parties of the 9th Royal Scots and 2/5th L.R.B. whose assistance enabled the defence of HUBNER FARM, a point very strongly held by the enemy, to be overcome and a large number of prisoners to be taken.
A SKETCH MAP (Marked "E") is attached which shows the dispositions of the attack at the moment that HUBNER FARM fell.
All this battalion's objectives were taken, held and handed over on relief.
MAP "C" attached shows the line of assembly and object-ives of each company and platoon

8. <u>RELIEF.</u>

The posts of this battalion were relieved on the night of the 21/22 September.
Relief commenced at about 7.45.pm but owing to heavy hostile shelling of HIBOU and neighbourhood and hostile counter attack was very considerable delayed. When the shelling quietened down the relief continued and was completed about 2.am
All the posts held by this battalion were shown to the relieving battalion (the 2/10th), who had, however, instructions from their Commanding Officer to take up

positions /

positions in advance of ours.
The Adjutant of the relieving battalion saw me in the afternoon for 5 minutes and took away a copy of my disposition Map and strength of posts.
No Officer of the relieving battalion came up to reconnoitre my posts before relief.
The accompanying Map "D" shews the disposition of my posts on relief.

4. COMMUNICATIONS

A. The original scheme of communications between Brigade Battle H.Q. (O.W.) and HIBOU (C) included armoured cable between ALBERTA and HIBOU (A) (W.G.) and also an elaborate ladder line. These were, however, completely smashed up before Zero, and although my Signal Officer and 4 linesmen were working on them all night, they never succeeded in getting any signals. Direct telephonic communication was therefore impossible, but communication with Brigade was satisfactorily maintained throughout by the following methods:-

(a) VISUAL. O.W. to W.G. - lamp communication both ways with Brigade Visual Station - O.Q.

(b) BY RUNNER RELAY system to ALBERTA (R.E.) and thence by wire to O.W.

(c) BY RUNNER RELAY system throughout to O.W.

(d) BY POWER BUZZER to ST JULIEN and thence by wire. This was working continuously.

B. From Captured positions to HIBOU (C)

This was entirely by runner and worked satisfactorily. The original scheme included communication with and through a Brigade Forward Signal Station at MARINE VIEW but this was smashed up.

C. AEROPLANES

A constant watch was kept for contact aeroplanes and counter attack aeroplanes. No messages were dropped at HIBOU or smoke balls observed.

D. DOGS

No dogs were sent to HIBOU (C).

E. PIGEONS.

Some messages were sent from HIBOU (C) duplicating Runner messages.

F./

F. FLAGS.

I consider that not sufficient use was made of flag signals by day. Flags could have been used with safety from my right and would have been visible.

G. LAMPS

I recommend that each company be provided with a "LUCAS" Lamp for signalling from captured positions. These to be taken up after positions captured and consolidated.

H. MESSAGE ROCKETS

were not used at all; they were retained in case o of emergency and were handed over on relief.

5. CASUALTIES

I regret to report 238 casualties O.R.s. :-

64 Killed
138 Wounded (including 5 at duty)
36 missing.

and officers 9;-

Killed.	2/Lieut SLOAN
Wounded.	2/Lieut CHANCELLOR
	2/Lieut RICHARDSON
	2/Lieut MORTIMER
	2/Lieut ROBINSON
	2/Lieut HITCH
	2/Lieut EDMONDS
Wounded & Missing.	2/Lieut BLANDE
	2/Lieut TAYLOR

Company strength on relief:-

Company	Officers.	O.R.s.
"A"	NIL	35
"B"	1	[illegible]
"C"	NIL	37
"D"	3	55
H.Q.	5	81
TOTAL	9	[illegible]

6. GENERAL REMARKS.

(a) I cannot praise too highly the zeal and determination of the men and officers or the exceptionally high standard of discipline of the battalion. A noteworthy feature was the large number of men and officers who carried on after being wounded, continued the attack and took part in consolidation until all the battalion's objectives were taken.

(b) A list of recommendations for honours and awards has already been submitted.

(c) All the wounded that could be found were collected and evacuated by the battalion S.B's who worked magnificently; a few wounded were collected by R.A.M.C. orderlies.

d./

(d) PRISONERS OF WAR & BOOTY

(i) At a low estimate the number of unwounded prisoners sent to our lines exceeds 180. I myself saw two parties of over 40 each come from my right and I have the testimony of 4 officers as to the number coming from HUBNER FARM, one of whom actually counted 70 and then had to attend to his gun and so could not count the rest. In addition ~~4~~ two unwounded officers were taken, plus 2 medical officers and 2 wounded officers.
It was impossible to send escorts. No unwounded man was allowed as escort and the enemy easily outran the wounded escort in their desire to get well behind our lines.

(ii) Killed by rifle, bayonet or bomb (i.e. otherwise than by our barrage) well over 100.

(iii) BOOTY:-
2 Heavy M.G.s by "A" Company
2 Heavy M.G.s) by "C" "
& 3 Light M.G.s)
1 Heavy M.G.) by "B" "
& 4 Light M.G.s)
3 Heavy M.G.s by "D" "

Total. 8 Heavy M.G.s and 8 L.G.s.

5. TOUCH was easily maintained both on the flanks and between companies.

6. POINTS NOTED FROM THE OPERATIONS

(i) It was possible to keep within 30 yards and in many instances 20 or even 10 yards of the barrage and it was very necessary to do so to deal successfully with fortified shell holes.

(ii) Any one or two determined men rushing one fortified shell hole can clear it with a bayonet. This was done in several instances.

(iii) Four men can take a PILL BOX by fire and movement, but more than four should be detailed for the job on account of probable casualties.

(iv) Once the attack can outflank a fortified farm the defence cracks up (see the account of the attack on HUBNER FARM and the PROMENADE)

(v) Co-operation between platoons and between companies is invaluable.
In this battalion every platoon knew not only its own objective but those of the platoons on either flank and forward and the greatest assistance was rendered by intelligent co-operation.
e.g. 1. Platoons taking a first objective assisted those following through with covering fire.
2. Platoons wiped out before reaching their objectives, had their objectives taken by sections detached from other platoons.
3. Covering fire was given by one company to another attacking a fortified position.

(vi) Covering fire and a determined bayonet assault will break up any defence.

(vii) The enemy mainly relied on cross fire from heavy M.G.s and frontal from L.G.s.

(viii) Posts should be selected whth to the front and on the flanks of captured strong points, as the latter are invariably shelled by the enemy later on.

(ix) The important weapon is the rifle and bayonet, grenades were used on the right and but few bombs thrown. No "P" bombs were used at all.

(x) When a battalion is to use a duckboard track for assembly by night, the track should be patrolled and guides posted at gaps caused by shell holes and derelict tanks; much delay was caused by these obstacles.

D. <u>WIRE</u> Hostile wire afforded no material obstacle.

F. <u>MAPS.</u> Attached:-

A. Copy of captured enemy disposition map.
B. Sketch of dispositions at moment of capture of HUBNER FARM
C. MAP showing line of assembly and objectives of platoons.
D. Disposition of posts handed over on relief.

G. <u>ARTILLERY</u>

The barrages both during the attack and enemy counter attacks were beyond all praise and completely satisfied all ranks.

H. <u>MACHINE GUNS</u>

The M.G. Sections attached to my battalion did excellent work, getting their guns into position in captured strong points with great promptitude. Use was made by them of captured enemy guns, for which there was a profusion of ammunition.

I. <u>TANKS.</u>

Owing to the rain the previous night the ground became very greasy on the surface. Tanks were, consequently not able to offer much assistance.

K. <u>S.A.A. & WATER</u>

Were collected off all dead and walking wounded cases, so that there was throughout a plentiful supply for this battalion. A convoy under 2/Lt LAMB brought up 21 tins of water, Very Lights and S.A.A. to "C" Company's H.Q., all of which was handed over to the relieving battalion.

I have the honour to remain,

Sir, your obedient servant.

Lieut-Colonel.
Commanding 2/8th Battalion. London Regiment.

In the Field.
25.9.17.

8 1714/58

Instructions regarding War Diaries and Intelligence Summaries are contained in F. S. Regs., Part II. and the Staff Manual respectively. Title pages will be prepared in manuscript.

WAR DIARY
or
~~INTELLIGENCE SUMMARY.~~
(Erase heading not required.)

Army Form C. 2118.

2/8 Bn City of London Regt.
Oct 1st to Oct 31st

Vol 10

Place	Date	Hour	Summary of Events and Information	Remarks and references to Appendices
LANDRETHUN	1.		Capt G.G. BARNES rejoined from senior officers Course.	
			At the funeral of M. LOUIS RINGOT a veteran of the war of 1870, who had served with the 110 Inf Regt; the Bn provided a firing party & buglers. RFJ	
	2.		2/Lieut R.F. ROTHWELL (22nd QUEENS) joined the Bn in the field. RFJ.	
	3.		2/Lieut E.E.L. TINSLEY rejoined from hospital. RFJ.	
			2/Lieut R.E. TWEEDLE joined the Bn in the field. RFJ.	
	4		Lt Col DERVICHE JONES MC went on leave to England.	
			2/Lieut C.S. ARMSTRONG evacuated sick to hosp. RFJ.	
	8th		Capt. Massy-Miles RAMC went on leave to England. RFJ.	
	5th		Major G.D. Hollis (Queens Own Glasgow Yeomanry) joined Bn in the field attached for instruction. RFJ.	
	9.		2/Lieut R.C. DUNCAN joined Bn in the field, also 106 OR as reinforcements RFJ	
			Capt J.A. Webster to England. RFJ.	
	11.		2/Lieut W.J. Ward to GHQ Small arms LG Course. ~~RFJ~~ Also 86 OR joined as reinforcements RFJ	
	12		Lt T.J. Mumford went on leave to England. 2/Lt R.F. Tugwell MC assumed duties of adjutant.	
			2/Lt R.F. ROTHWELL XIX Corps L.G. School. RFJ.	

Instructions regarding War Diaries and Intelligence Summaries are contained in F. S. Regs., Part II. and the Staff Manual respectively. Title pages will be prepared in manuscript.

WAR DIARY
or
~~INTELLIGENCE~~ SUMMARY.
(Erase heading not required.)

Army Form C. 2118.

2/8 Bn City of London Regt.

Oct 1st — Oct 31st

Place	Date	Hour	Summary of Events and Information	Remarks and references to Appendices
LANDRETHUN	14.		Capt A.D. Heaton M.C. went on leave to England.	
			Lt Col A.D. DERVICHE JONES DSO MC returned from leave.	
			Capt F.P. Wheeldon rejoined the Bn in the field from England (wounded) RMS	
POPERINGHE	20		The Bn moved to POPERINGHE. RMS	
	22.		Capt Massey-Miles RAMC returned from leave. RM	
	23.		2/Lt Brown took over duties of Divl Burials Officer while that Officer was on leave. RMS	
SIEGE Camp	24		The Bn moved to SIEGE Camp.	
	25		Major G.G. Barnes and Lieut TRegellis wounded by a bomb in a bombing raid and wounded [illegible]. Captn Rukes slightly wounded by the same bomb but remains at duty. JMM	
			Captain & Adjutant J.M. Mumford returned from leave JMM	
CANAL BANK	26		The Battalion moves to the Canal Bank Ypres. JMM	
YPRES	29		The Battalion moves to KEMPTON PARK CAMP at 11 A.M. JMM	
			The Battalion moves to place of assembly for attack leaving KEMPTON PARK at 8 P.M. JMM	

T2134. Wt. W708–776. 500000. 4/15. Sir J. C. & S.

Instructions regarding War Diaries and Intelligence Summaries are contained in F. S. Regs., Part II. and the Staff Manual respectively. Title pages will be prepared in manuscript.

WAR DIARY
or
~~INTELLIGENCE SUMMARY.~~
(Erase heading not required.)

Army Form C. 2118.

2/8th Battalion City of London Regt.

Place	Date	Hour	Summary of Events and Information	Remarks and references to Appendices
	1917 October			
V.19.a.7.1.	30th		The Battalion attacked S.E. of POELCAPPELE at 5.50 AM. Orders for attack and report on operations attached as appendix. JHM	No. 1 + 2
SEIGE CAMP	31		The Battalion was relieved on night of 30th/31st and proceeded to SEIGE CAMP. Casualties:- Killed Captain F.P. WHEELDON 2/Lt P.C. DUNCAN O.R. 34. Wounded and missing 2/Lt R. McALISTER, Captn E.B. BARNETT, 2/Lt R.G. BARNES 2/Lt E.C.T. FINCH 2/Lt A PEACOCK. 2/Lt E.E.L. TINSLEY (19th Bn London Regt). O.R. 214. Wounded at duty Lt R.N. Shapley, 2/Lt H Book. O.R. 3 JHM	

J.H. [illegible] Captn [illegible]
[stamp] [illegible] (P.O. RIFLES)

A. D. Derviche-Jones
Lt Col.
Commanding 2/8th BATTN. LONDON REGT. (P.O. RIFLES)

Instructions regarding War Diaries and Intelligence Summaries are contained in F. S. Regs., Part II. and the Staff Manual respectively. Title pages will be prepared in manuscript.

WAR DIARY
or
~~INTELLIGENCE SUMMARY.~~
(Erase heading not required.)

Army Form C. 2118.

2/8 City of London Regt.

Oct 1st — Oct 31st

Place	Date	Hour	Summary of Events and Information	Remarks and references to Appendices
			The following awards were made after the operations of 20th Sept.	
			Lt Col AD DERVICHE JONES MC. — DSO	
			Lt (a/capt) AD HEATON — MC.	
			Lt (a/capt) ER LANES — "	
			2Lt (a/capt) C. KELLY — "	
			2Lt RF TREGELLES — "	
			2Lt ES MORTIMER — "	
			2Lt GW CHANCELLOR — "	
			2Lt CS ARMSTRONG — "	
			2Lt HMW RICHARDSON. MC. — Bar to MC.	
			OR — DCM. 370625 Sgt. Francis, HJ.	
			" 370744 " Harris. G.H.	

T2134. Wt. W708—776. 500000. 4/15. Sir J. C. & S.

Army Form C. 2118.

Instructions regarding War Diaries and Intelligence Summaries are contained in F. S. Regs., Part II. and the Staff Manual respectively. Title pages will be prepared in manuscript.

WAR DIARY
or
~~INTELLIGENCE SUMMARY.~~
(Erase heading not required.)

2/8 City of London Regt.

Oct 1st – Oct 31st

Place	Date	Hour	Summary of Events and Information			Remarks and references to Appendices
			awards continued.			
			371311	Cpl Solomon . G . MM.	Bar to MM.	
			370979	Sgt Murray B.T.	MM.	
			370673	Cpl Seager G A (att. LTMB)	"	
			371397	L/Cpl Gibbs T.M.	"	
			371360	L/Cpl Needley . F.	"	
			372617	Rfn Dixon . W.	"	
			372548	" Mitchley B	"	
			372301	" Murphy . M.	"	
			372609	" Soper . J.	"	
			372547	" Wright . W.A.	"	
			385057	" TODD . A.	"	
			372806	" Sparkes . E.	"	
			372631	" Payne . E.	"	
			373116	" Ebbs . W.	"	
			371164	" Macintyre A.T.	"	
			370747	" Drew . H.J.	"	

T2134. Wt. W708–776. 500000. 4/15. Sir J. C. & S.

Instructions regarding War Diaries and Intelligence Summaries are contained in F. S. Regs., Part II. and the Staff Manual respectively. Title pages will be prepared in manuscript.

Army Form C. 2118.

WAR DIARY
or
~~INTELLIGENCE~~ SUMMARY.
(Erase heading not required.)

2/8 Bn. The City of London Regt.

Oct 1st – Oct 31st

Place	Date	Hour	Summary of Events and Information	Remarks and references to Appendices
			awards contin	
			372513. Rfn McKenzie F. MM.	
			372474 " Roper. F.V. "	
			385155 " White. A.R. (att LTMB) "	

T2134. Wt. W708–776. 500000. 4/15. Sir J. C. & S.

ROUGH SKETCH SHEWING DISPOSITIONS
BEFORE HUBNER FARM FELL

Ref. POELCAPPELLE
1/10.000.

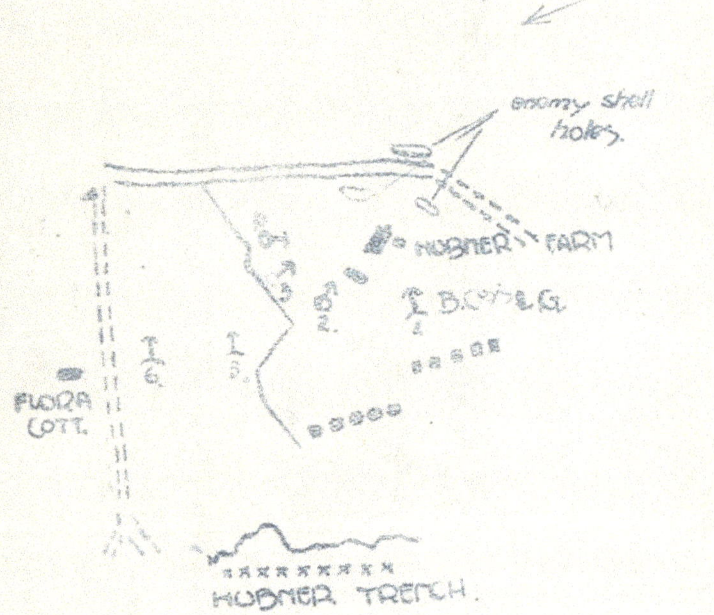

1. B.Coy. L.G. engaging it frontally
2. D. " Corporal and 4 men.
3. 3. Scots Party (6)
4. 4. L.Q.B. men well on LEFT FLANK.
5. } 16 Platoon which afterwards formed posts D11. and 12.
6. }

ENEMY DISPOSITIONS OF THE PROMENADE

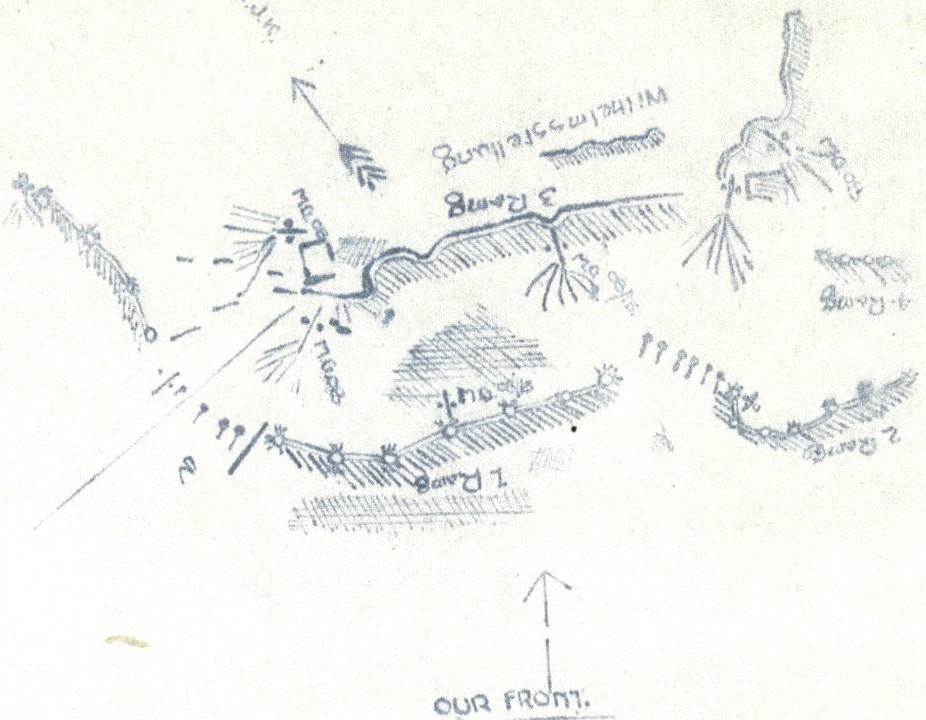

OUR FRONT.

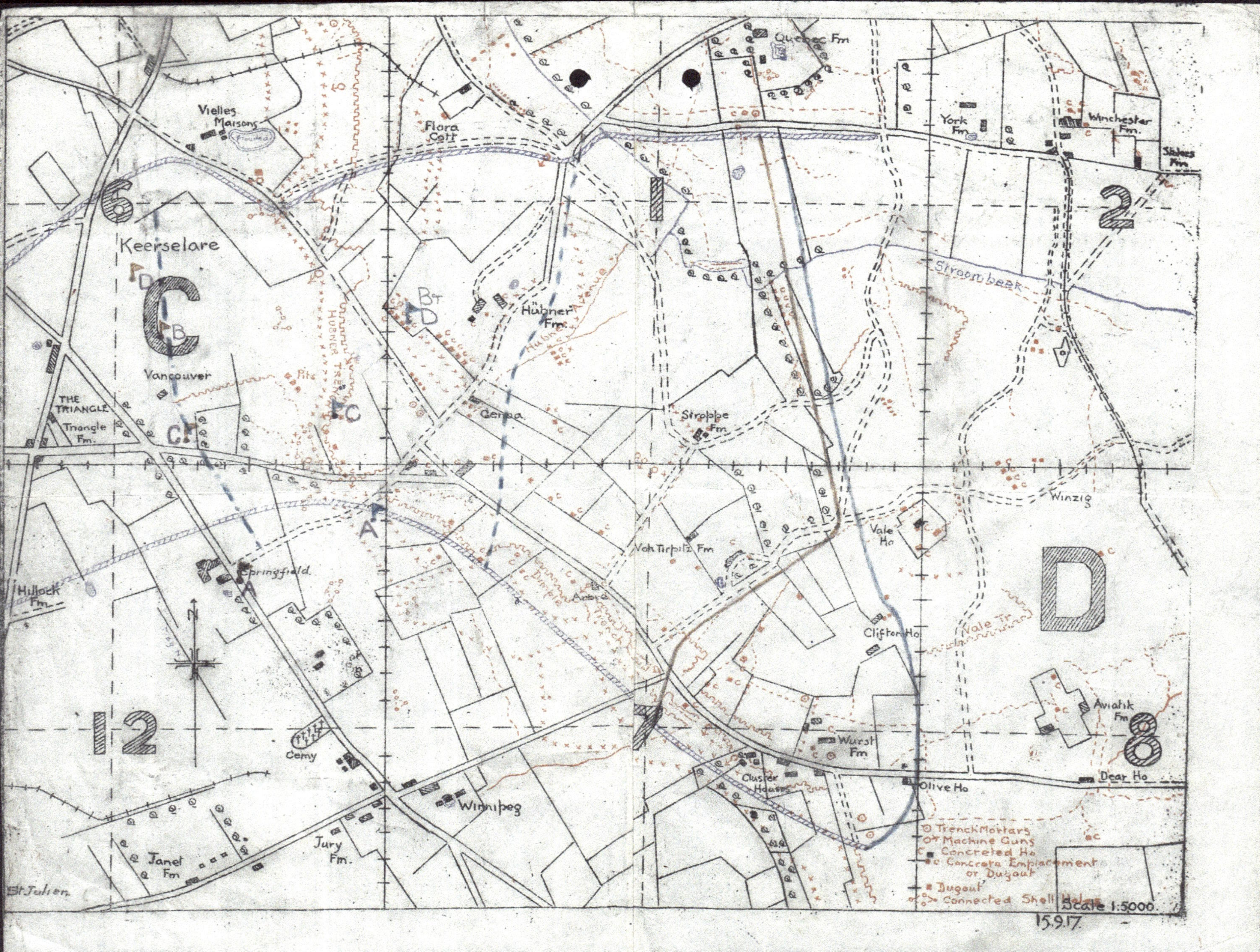

Quebec Fm
Vielles Maisons
Flooded
Flora Cott
York Fm
Winchester Fm.
Stokes Fm
Keerselare
Stroombeek
Hubner Fm
Hubner Avenue
Hubner Trench
Vancouver
THE TRIANGLE
Triangle Fm.
Pits
Genoa
Stroppe Fm
Winzig
Vale Ho
Von Tirpitz Fm
Springfield
Hillock Fm
Dimple Trench
Clifton Ho
Vale Tr
Aviatik Fm
Wurst Fm
Dear Ho
Olive Ho
Cluster Houses
Cemy
Winnipeg
Jury Fm.
Janet Fm
St Julien
Trench Mortars
Machine Guns
Concreted Ho
Concrete Emplacement or Dugout
Dugout
Connected Shell Holes
Scale 1:5000
15.9.17.

Copy No: 13

SECRET.   [illegible] Bn. The London Regiment.

OPERATION ORDERS No:7.

Ref: Sheet 28.N.W.
[illegible]
[illegible] 1/20,000.
[illegible]
SPECIAL [illegible].

---

1. The attack on the enemy is to be resumed on a date which has been communicated verbally to Company Commanders at an hour to be notified later.

2. (a) The [illegible]th Infantry Brigade will be attacking with one battalion (the [illegible])

(b) The [illegible] will co-operate on the left and a battalion of the [illegible] Division will attack on the right of this battalion and will be holding the present outpost line.

3. The objectives of the [illegible] are:-
(a) CAMERON HOUSES.
(b) [illegible] FARM.
(c) [illegible] FARM & [illegible] HOUSES.

4. The objectives of Companies are as follows:-
(a) On the Left.- B. Company. CAMERON HOUSES.
A. Company. the trench marked A in a blue oval, this trench is believed to be either a sunken road or a fortified trench and is known to contain a strong force of the enemy.

(b) On the Right.- D. Company. [illegible] HOUSES and the area marked [illegible].
C. Company. [illegible] FARM & [illegible] FARM.

5. The attack will be made in two phases:-
1st Phase:- The dotted red line, on which the creeping barrage will pause for [illegible] minutes.
2nd Phase:- The solid red line, in front of which a protector will be [illegible] (see Barrage)

6. ASSEMBLY.
(a) The battalion will assemble along taped lines on a two company front.

(b) The leading Company's on the line marked in pencil on the special map.

(c) Each company will have two platoons in front and two platoons in rear.

(d) Companies will assemble from front to rear:-
On the left. B. - A.
On the Right D. - C.

(e) O/C ASSEMBLY:- Captain [illegible] M.C.
ASSEMBLY H.Q.:- [illegible]

(f) [illegible]:- 1 officer and [illegible] other ranks from each company.
Platoon Guides:- [illegible] other Rank from each platoon carrying a disc with the number of his platoon.
[illegible] Guides:- An officer [illegible] and [illegible] of [illegible] Company.

[illegible]

(g) After taping completed:-
  i. The taping party will remain on their respective Company tapes.
  ii. The platoon guides will return to MEUNIER HILL where they will meet platoons as they arrive. Each platoon guide will conduct his own platoon to his platoon position of assembly. Platoon guides to be at MEUNIER HILL by 8.30. p.m.

(h) The Battalion must be in position by 3. a.m. Y.- Z night.

(k) Covering parties:-
  i. Arrangements are being made for the 7/6th to provide covering parties for the taping of the line of assembly.
  ii. C. & D. Companies will find covering parties for the assembly.
  iii. Covering parties will take up a position about 30 yards in front of the taping line and will consist of 1 Rifle Section per leading company.

(l) All arrangements for:-
  i. ROUTE GUIDES.
  ii. Taping and
  iii. Assembly

are under the direction of O/C Assembly who is responsible that the battalion is duly assembled at the time named.

(m) ROUTE GUIDES of A. Company will fall in at the rear of A. Company as the rear platoon of this Company passes the guides. It is suggested that these guides should be selected from the rear platoon of A. Company.

(n) (a) All platoons will proceed via. V.19.a.7.3. (Bn. H.Q.) to MEUNIER HILL to pick up their guides.
  (b) MEUNIER HILL will be marked by a red lamp.
  (c) THAMES FARM will be marked by a green lamp.
  (d) Special men will be detailed by the Signalling officer to look after these lamps. These men will get their instructions from Signalling officer and will proceed up the line with him.

(o) (a) Order of march from KEMPTON PARK:-
  H.Q. - D. C. - B. - A.
  (b) Time:- Y 6. p.m.
  (c) 100 yards between platoons.
  (d) Administrative arrangements see separate order.

V. DISPOSITIONS & FORMATIONS.

(a) The Battalion will attack on a two company front. These fronts have been selected so as to afford the best ground for companies and to avoid swamps and bad going.

(b) Each Company will be formed up on a two platoon front.

(c) Each Company will have one platoon as Company Commanders Reserve. This reserve should not be involved in the initial fighting but be kept fresh for contingencies.

Contd.

d.

(d) Each Company will advance with one Section of each of its leading platoons extended and remaining sections in file: rear platoons of Companies in two lines of Sections.

8. PLAN OF ATTACK:-
This has already been explained to Company Commanders. Shortly it is as follows:-
(a) On right:-
i. Two platoons of D. Company take [illegible] HOUSES - One platoon swings through to the left to enfilade the trench track in V.21.A. and protect the flank of troops detailed to attack [illegible] & HINTON - One platoon in Company Commanders reserve.
ii. C. Company leapfrogs over D. One platoon attacks [illegible] and one platoon HINTON. One platoon supports these attacks. One platoon in Company Commanders reserve.

(b) On left:-
i. Two platoons of B. Company attack CAMERON frontally: one platoon advances on right flank prepared to give covering fire on Trench track and to outflank right [illegible] of CAMERON. One platoon in Company Commanders reserve.
ii. A. Company leapfrogs over B. Company and attacks TRENCH Track with two platoons. One platoon supports right and is prepared to co-operate in attack on [illegible] on the right flank of PAPA. One platoon in Company Commanders reserve.

9. STRONG POINTS.
(a) by D. Company at [illegible] HOUSES.

(b) by C. Company by [illegible] FARM and at HINTON FARM.

(c) by B. Company at CAMERON HOUSES
to provide frontal and flank defence garrison of each strong point - one platoon.

10. LEWIS GUNS.
(a) 8 Lewis Guns with teams of 4 men each (two guns and teams from each Company) will go in the line. The remaining guns and the trained Lewis Gunners of each team will go to Details Camp.

(b) Of the 8 battle L.G. teams and guns, the two of B. Company and the two of D. Company will remain at Bn. H.Q. as Bn. Commanders reserve.

(c) Two of A. Company will proceed with A. Company to [illegible] HILL and obtain the best cover obtainable until 45 minutes after Zero when they will move to the [illegible] - [illegible] road and along there to a point on this road near CAMERON HOUSES. These two guns are intended to deal with enemy counter attacks from the front or either flank.

Contd.
4.

(d) Of C. Company's guns one gun and team will advance with and under the orders of O.C. C. Company and take up a position at MORAY HOUSE. The other gun will proceed with C. Company to [illegible] FARM and await instructions of O.C. C. Company.

(e) Riflemen attached to L.G. teams other than as above mentioned are returned to their Rifle Sections.

11. M.G.s.

(a) Two Vickers guns will be in readiness at GLOSTER FARM. When the situation allows O.C. C. Coy. or the senior officer of attacking troops will send a message to GLOSTER FM for these guns to move up, one to MORAY and one to HINTON.

(b) Two Vickers guns will be in the neighbourhood of Bn. H.Q. Messages for their assistance must be sent to O.C. 8/6th Bn.

12. BARRAGE.

(a) The attack is preceded by a bombardment for 48 hours by Corps Artillery.

(b) A creeping barrage will open at Zero 200 yards in front of assembly line and halts there for 6 minutes while assaulting troops advance.

(c) Barrage lifts 50 yards at a time, halting at each lift for 6 minutes.

(d) A protector barrage will be laid in front of the dotted red line for 3 minutes

(e) Barrage will then lift 40 yards at a time until solid red line is reached.

(f) A protector barrage will stand 150 yards in front of solid red line for

13. LIAISON.

(a) As soon as GARRON HOUSES are taken B. Company will establish a post, 1 N.C.O. and 6 men, on the [illegible] Road until the L.G.s. detailed relieve it. This post will then get in touch with the 8/6th on the left of this road and report position of right post of 8/6th.

(b) Owing to the swampy ground on the right, it will not be possible to establish direct contact with the Battalion on the right flank. Endeavour must be made to see and report where their nearest post is.

Sheet 2.

14. COMMUNICATIONS.

A. To Bn. H.Q.

(a) Advance visual and runners relay post at [illegible] HILL where the Bn. Sig. Officer will be stationed. Direct communication will be made from there to Bn. H.Q. and GLOSTER FM.

(b) B. Company will establish a LUCAS Lamp at CAMERON HOUSES after this objective has been taken and transmit also for A. Company.

(c) C. Company will establish a LUCAS Lamp at [illegible] (when taken) and transmit also for D. Co.

(d) Signallers of all companies will use all means of keeping in continuous touch with [illegible].

(e) i. Company runners direct to [illegible].
ii. Runners messages will be relayed to Bn. H.Q.
iii. Messages which are not important should be sent by visual and not by runner.
Other messages both by runner and visual.
iv. Each company on taking up position to send 4 runners to [illegible], 2 of these will return to their companies.
v. The one runner per company at present with with Bn. H.Q. will remain with Bn. H.Q. and act as Bn. runner.

B. To Brigade.

(a) By Wire via PHEASANT FARM.
(b) By LUCAS Lamp to PHEASANT FARM.
(c) By runner relay post at PHEASANT FARM.
(d) By Power Buzzer.
(e) By Pigeons.

15. MEDICAL ARRANGEMENTS.

(a) R.A.P. at Bn. H.Q. (V.[illegible].a.7.1.)
(b) [illegible] R.A.M.C. Squads will carry back from Bn.H.Q. to PHEASANT FARM.
(c) S.B.s. of the [illegible]/5th will assist S.B.s. of the [illegible]/5th in clearing the front of wounded.
(d) Walking wounded via R.A.P. or GLOSTER FARM to [illegible].

16. HEADQUARTERS.

(a) Bn. H.Q. at V.16. a. 7. 1. shared with [illegible]/5th
(b) Advanced Bn. Report Centre, [illegible].
(c) B. & A. Companies will establish Company H.Q. at CAMERON HOUSES.
ii. C. Company at [illegible] FARM.
iii. D. Company at [illegible] HOUSES.

(d) Brigade at VARNA FARM.

17. TIME.

Watches will be synchronised at Bn. H.Q. CANAL BANK at [illegible], and again before leaving [illegible] FM.

18. Administrative Orders issued separately.

Lieut. - Colonel.
Commanding. [illegible]/5th Bn., The [illegible] Regt.

[illegible]

APPENDIX 2 File

Headquarters

174th Infantry Brigade

Preliminary Report on OPERATIONS of
30th October, 1917.

----

1. ASSEMBLY. This required the most careful organisation, as owing to the short notice of the plan of attack, reconnaissance had only been possible the previous night, and also as a relief was taking place that night, no guides other than our own were available.

A. The organisation was as follows :-

i. O.C. Assembly Captain C. KELLY.

ii. Taping party. 1 Officer and 2 O.R's from each Company.

iii. Route Guides. 1 Sergeant and 10 O.R's to mark places where men might go astray up to Bn.H.Q. V.18.a.7.1. and from there to where the Battalion struck across country to MEUNIER.

iv. Platoon Guides. One O.R. from each platoon with a numbered disc. These accompanied the taping party and when they had planted their discs returned to MEUNIER to meet their platoons.

v. H.Q. Assembly :- MEUNIER.

vi. An advanced party of the Signalling Officer and 4 men to establish a red hurricane lamp at MEUNIER and a blue lamp at TRACAS.
Note :- These proved invaluable as guiding marks.

B. The result was that in spite of heavy hostile shelling and forming up on a tape on unknown ground, the whole battalion was formed up with less than 20 casualties within 8 hours of leaving KEMPTON PARK.

C. Great credit is due to Captain KELLY for the organisation and carrying out of the Assembly.

D. The brilliant moon was a drawback as well as useful for the Assembly as it seems certain that the enemy perceived men coming up.
Heavy M.G. fire opened from the enemy across the assembly places at 11 pm and the enemy barraged and bombarded from the BREWERY to the LEKKERBOTER BEEK from 3 to 4.30 am.

2. ~~xx~~. The Assembly Troops were visited before ZERO and all found to be cheerful and in good condition.

3. BARRAGE.

(a) Our Artillery Barrage started at 5.42 am.

(b) The M.G. Barrage at 5.41 am.

(c) The barrage was not sufficient to keep down the Boche M.G. fire or the Boche themselves. From the start Boche were observed in TRACK Trench firing and watching; there was scarcely a moment they were not seen in this place (see Map herewith) from Zero

onward

onward and our barrage did not affect them.

(d) Owing to the condition of the ground the barrage was too quick. Our troops started in most places <u>before</u> the barrage, but never caught it up in any place.

(e) All the men who were in the Action of the 20th September as well as in this Action say that the barrage was weak and nothing like so good as on the 20th September.

(f) Boche barrage started at 5.44 am., came down just on our taped line and crept back towards and with our barrage. It was a weak barrage but caused some casualties.
It crept right back to PAPA FARM. On the right 80 % of the casualties were caused by this barrage.

(g) From 3 am to 4.30 am Boche bombarded the BREWERY and POELCAPELLE generally with 6.9's. This district, MEUNIER and TRACAS received special treatment then and from Zero onwards. Capt KELLY was unable to get back to H.Q. until 11.0.am though his job was completed about 3.0. am.
From Bn.H.Q. to PHEASANT FARM came under Boche barrage at 12.30 am - 2.30 am (heavy) and 5.45.

4. <u>STATE of GROUND.</u>

(a) From reconnaissance by my officers from MEUNIER and TRACAS and from information from 173rd Bde it was hoped to find fair going on the right and also on the left in places.

(b) Unfortunately this proved incorrect. In all places men were up to their knees, thighs or waists in every step taken. Rifles which were uncovered (for covering fire) were useless after the first 50 yards; others were kept wrapt up for a long time in case the objectives were reached and could not be used for fire.

(c) No man could get a fair foot hold anywhere and most were slipping over into shell holes. By the greatest determination positions were reached at places marked on map by a few, very few men. Posts were established at other places also marked.

(d) It was quite impossible to get up to the barrage and any one getting up to go forward was subjected to M.G. fire and rifle fire. Where sections kept together the whole section was hit.

(e) The mud was thick and sticky and the men were exhausted before advancing 100 yards.

(f) The best going and that bad but possibly passable was on the left towards CAMERON HOUSE.

(g) Some men got forward and ultimately were relieved by crawling on all fours in the mud; they were too done up to walk through the mud.

5. <u>ENEMY M.G. FIRE AND SNIPING.</u>

(a) M.G's from V.27.b.60.60. (direction)
V.27.a.90.95. (reported)
V.21.d.10.60. (located)
V.21.d.00.80. (located)
V.21.a.05.95. (located)
V.21.a.80.40. (direction)
V.21.a.40.50. (located)
V.21.a.20.60. (direction)
V.21.d.45.38. (direction)

(b) <u>Snipers.</u>
Up a tree at V.20.d.05.95. along TRACK Trench as marked

marked on Map : V.21.a.70.70. through MORAY House to V.21.d.90.40.

6. Enemy fired through our barrage and their own creeping back barrage both with rifle and M.G.'s.

7. LIMIT OF ADVANCE.
   (a) On right. to V.21.c.90.40 and V.21.c.70.80. Posts were not established at these places, as only one or two men and an officer got here. Posts were established at V.21.c.60.80 and V.21.c.60.50
   (b) On left. About V.21.a.00.90., V.21.a.00.62., and V.20.b.80.40 where small posts were established.

None of these posts were consolidated, as the nature of the ground made this impossible, but they were held until relief.

8. COMMUNICATIONS.
   (a) An advanced Report Centre was established at MEUNIER and visual kept up from there to Bn.H.Q. throughout.
   (b) The failure to get messages from Companies was due to the ground. Many messages sent by officers never got back to MEUNIER at all, the messenger being hit by hostile M.G's or rifles, others were 6 to 7 hours late in arriving at MEUNIER.
   Nearly all the Company Signallers were hit. The first message was brought back by a man crawling through the mud the whole way on all fours - he was utterly exhausted and many hours late.

9. GENERALLY.
   (a) The ground was the enemy and gave Boche easy targets whenever a man stood up.
   (b) The barrage was ineffective, probably due to soft ground.
   (c) Oblique hostile M.G. fire very effective.
   (d) L.G's. The only one brought into action was useless in three minutes; all uncovered rifles ditto; all covered rifles ditto within 10 minutes of being uncovered.
   (e) If they advanced upright, they were an easy target, if on all fours the men were exhausted in a few minutes.
   (f) No outflanking movement was possible for above reasons
   (g) On this sort of ground men must be extended; where sections were together the whole section was wiped out.
   (h) If CAMERON HOUSE could be taken, a flank attack towards PAPA and HINTON would in my opinion be successful and easy.

10. CASUALTIES.

Estimated

8 Officers
240 O.R.

Lieut.-Col.
Commanding 2/8th Bn., The London Regt.

31.10.17.

Sheet [illegible].

Issued [illegible].1[illegible].17. at [illegible].[illegible] . m.

Copy No: 1. Commanding Officer.
2. Captain C. [illegible].
3. O.C. "A" Co.
4. O.C. B. Co.
5. O.C. C. Co.
6. O.C. D. Co.
7. Adjutant.
8. Sig. Officer.
9. Bde.
10. "
11. O.C. [illegible]/[illegible]th Bn.
12. O.C. [illegible] M.G.Co.
13. War Diary.

ADMINISTRATIVE INSTRUCTIONS. 28.10.17.

1. DRESS. LIGHT Battle Order - Haversack on back - entrenching tool in front - Leather jerkin worn - 1 full waterbot.

1 bomb per man in Haversack.
1 Ground Flare GREEN per man in pocket.
S.A.A. all ranks 50 rounds unless otherwise ordered.
L.G. S.A.A. only 1 magazine in each pannier instead of two.
Iron ration in haversack.
Rifle and bayonet.
Mess Tin.

2. STORES. FLARES. Ground Flares Red will be exchanged for ground flares Green at Divisional Dump POND FARM at
SHOVELS - 25 per company will be returned to Divisional Dump POND FARM at
Shovels 13 per Company will be stacked near cookers.
Sandbags will be stacked near cookers.
Bombs - S.A.A. Iron Rations are already in possession.
Haversacks and Leather jerkins will arrive this afternoon and will be drawn from Dump near Cookers at
Surplus S.A.A. Packs and all surplus kit including Company Stores other than Very Pistols, ammunition and S.O.S. rockets will be stacked by Companies near Cookers at 8.30. am. tomorrow.

3. KIT. No kit (except Very pistols, very pistol ammunition and S.O.S. rockets) other than as laid down in para 1 will be carried as men must go into battle as lightly equipped as possible.

4. MARKINGS. A X will be painted on the outside of haversack of each man before leaving the CANAL BANK under Company arrangements, dimensions each line 4 inches long by 1 inch broad. Paint and a brush will be issued to Companies as soon as available.

Colours: A. Company. RED.
B. Company. BLACK.
C. Company. ~~WHITE.~~ Yellow
D. Company. Blue

5. MOVE. Companies must be prepared to move to KEMPTON PRK by 10. am. tomorrow.

6. ACCOMMODATION.
Accommodation in CANAL BANK must be scraped and left clean.

7. DISCIPLINE. The importance of strict water and food discipline must be impressed on all ranks as ground is bad and more water and food will not be available after leaving KEMPTON PARK.

T.J.MUMFORD.
Captain & Adjutant.

Instructions regarding War Diaries and Intelligence Summaries are contained in F. S. Regs., Part II. and the Staff Manual respectively. Title pages will be prepared in manuscript.

1748/58

WAR DIARY
~~or~~
~~INTELLIGENCE~~ SUMMARY.
(Erase heading not required.)

Army Form C. 2118.

2/8 Bat London Regt
Nov 1 – 30 1917

Vol 11

Place	Date	Hour	Summary of Events and Information	Remarks and references to Appendices
SIEGE CAMP	Nov 1		Maj. G.D. HOLLIS to Hospital. Lt A. MOON rejoined Bat from 168 Inf. Brigade. a.m	
	Nov 5		Lt C.A. MONTGOMERY rejoined Bat from 3rd Army Sniping School a.m.	
CANAL BANK YPRES	Nov 6		Batn moved to CANAL BANK YPRES and were employed on working parties a.m.	
	Nov 8		Capt. T.A.B PURKIS proceeded on 14 days leave to England a.m.	
	Nov 10		2 Lt G E LOCKE and 2nd Lt P.E D'ARCY joined the Bat in the Field a.m.	
	Nov 11		Capt A.C. SOUTON joined the Bat from 2/11 London Regt and assumed the duties of 2nd in Command a.m	
	Nov 12		2nd Lt D.W. LAMB proceeded to England on 14 days leave. Lt R.J. KEENE proceeded to HAVRES on duty a.m	
SIEGE CAMP	Nov 15		Batn moved to SIEGE CAMP a.m	
HERZEELE	Nov 17		Batn moved to HERZEELE and went into Billets. Battle surplus rejoined the Batn.	
			2nd Lt R R POULTON and 2nd Lt W.B SCARTH joined the Bat. a.m	
	Nov 24		2nd Lt G.E. LOCKE proceeded to Fifth Army Assistant Adjutants Musketry Course a.m.	
PROVEN	Nov 25		Bat moved by march route to PROVEN a.m.	
SENINGHEM	Nov 26		Bn moved by train & march route to billets at SENINGHEM and AFFRINGUES a.m	
			Capt T.A.B. PURKIS rejoined the Bat after 14 days leave a.m	
ARLETTE	Nov 27		Batn marched to billets at ARLETTE a.m.	
	Nov 28		Lt Col. A.D. DERVICHE JONES M.C. D.S.O. proceeded to XVIII Corps Open Warfare Course	
			Major A.C. SOUTON assumed command of the Bat. a.m	
ESCOEUILLES	Nov 29		Batn marched into billets at ESCOEUILLES and SUCRES a.m.	

D. D. & L., London, E.C.
(A7883) Wt. W809/M1672 350,000 4/17 Sch. 52a Forms/C/2118/14

Instructions regarding War Diaries and Intelligence Summaries are contained in F. S. Regs., Part II. and the Staff Manual respectively. Title pages will be prepared in manuscript.

WAR DIARY ~~or~~ ~~INTELLIGENCE~~ SUMMARY.

(*Erase heading not required.*)

2/8 Bat. London Regt.

Nov 1 – 30 1917

Army Form C. 2118.

Place	Date	Hour	Summary of Events and Information	Remarks and references to Appendices
			The following awards were made after the operations of October 30th	
			Military Cross	
			Capt G. E. GUNNING	
			Capt A. J. PERRY C. 7.	
			Military Medals	
			371653 Pte Roberson D. A.	
			371244 L/C Armstrong H.	
			371593 Pte Board J. E	
			372434 Pte Bacon W. A.	
			385158 Pte Bray T. V.	
			371623 Pte McDermott M. J.	
			370061 Serjt Fisher J. H.	
			370029 Pte Kaltan H. A.	

VICTORIA CROSS

The above honour was awarded to Serjt KNIGHT A. J. B Company for services rendered in the operations of Sept 20th.

A. Moore Lt

[signature] Capt & Adjt
for Lt Col Commanding
2/8 Bn London Regt.

D. D. & L., London, E.C.
(A7883) Wt. W809/M1672 350,000 4/17 Sch. 52a Forms/C/2118/14

Instructions regarding War Diaries and Intelligence Summaries are contained in F. S. Regs., Part II. and the Staff Manual respectively. Title pages will be prepared in manuscript.

WAR DIARY
or
INTELLIGENCE SUMMARY.
(Erase heading not required.)

Army Form C. 2118.

2/8 Bat. London Regt

VII 12

Place	Date	Hour	Summary of Events and Information	Remarks and references to Appendices
ESCOEUILLES	Dec 1		Lt Col A.D. DERVICHE JONES M.C. D.S.O. rejoined the Batn from XVIII Corps C.Os Course	
			Sapping Platoon 2 N.C.Os and 28 men formed under Lt MOON	
			Sniping Section 2 N.C.Os and 10 men formed under Lt MONTGOMERY A.M.	
	Dec 2		Lt D.W. LAMB rejoined the Batn from 14 days leave to England A.M.	
			2nd Lt R.E. Tweedall proceeded on Inf. Course II Corps. Battalion training under Coy arrangements. Night Patrols etc.	CAM
	DEC 5		2nd Lt. W.B. SCARTH proceeded to II Corps Bombing Course. CAM.	
BAYENGHAM	DEC. 7		Battalion moved to BAYENGHEM. CAM.	
	Dec. 8		Battalion marched to WIZERNES + Trained to ELVERDINGHE - Light Rlwy to KEMPTON PARK. - C. and D Coys	CAM
KEMPTON PARK			marched to PHEASANT TRENCH and took over from 15 CHESHIRE REGT. Remainder of Battn relieved 15 Cheshire	CAM
			Regt at KEMPTON PARK. Battalion attached to 175 Inf. Bde. C.A.M.	
	Dec. 9		Battalion preparing to go into the line. Dispositions of 2/10 London Regt obtained by Intelligence Officer. C.A.M.	
IN The Line	Dec 10	4.00pm	Battalion relieved 2/10 London Regt in POELCAPELLE Sector. A Coy suffered 12 O.R. Casualties. remainder	CAM
			of relief quiet. CAM. Major A.C. SOUTTEN M.C. assumed command vice Lt Col DERACHE-JONES M.C. D.S.O. CAM.	
	Dec 11		Battalion holding line. CAM. Lt. R.N. SHAPLEY rejoined from leave. CAM.	
	Dec 12	7.30pm	2/12 London Regt relieved 2/8 Battalion in POELCAPELLE Sector. Battalion marched out to CANAL BANK	CAM
			via KEMPTON PARK. - At KEMPTON PARK 8 O.R.S suffered casualties from Shrapnel. C.A.M.	
CANAL BANK	Dec 13		Battalion resting at CANAL BANK. CAM. Lieut. J. A. BOSTOCK to be CAPTAIN from Aug 15 - 1917 C.A.M.	
	Dec 14		Battalion resting at CANAL BANK. CAM. [Captain C.E. GUNNING M.C. rejoined from leave	CAM

D. D. & L., London, E.C. (A7883) Wt. W809/M672 350,000 4/17 Sch. 52a Forms/C/2118/14

Instructions regarding War Diaries and Intelligence Summaries are contained in F. S. Regs., Part II, and the Staff Manual respectively. Title pages will be prepared in manuscript.

WAR DIARY
or
INTELLIGENCE SUMMARY.
(Erase heading not required.)

Army Form C. 2118.

Place	Date	Hour	Summary of Events and Information	Remarks and references to Appendices
CANAL BANK	DEC 15		Lt. Col. D.A. DERVICHE JONES DSO.M.C. assumed command of 174 Inf Bde. Battalion furnishing WORKING PARTIES Cam	
do	DEC 16		LIEUT. T. J. MUMFORD proceeded to V ARMY Musketry COURSE. Lt MONTGOMERY temporary Adjutant. Cam.	
	18.		2nd Lt. LOCKE rejoined from Course. Cam.	
do	19		Captain. H.W. PRIESTLEY rejoined the Battalion and assumed duty of ADJUTANT. Cam.	
	20		Major A.C. SOUTTEN. M.C. proceeded on leave. CAPT. H.W. PRIESTLEY assumed Command of Battalion. Lt C.A. MONTGOMERY Cam	
			assumed duty of Adjutant. 2nd Lt. W.C. BRUGGEMEYER joined the Battalion. Cam.	
do	21		2nd Lt. W.B. SCARTH rejoined Battalion from II Corps Bombing Course. Cam.	
	22.		2nd Lt. A.G. ODDLAFSON and 2nd Lt. J.M. ELAM joined the Battalion from Reserve Battalion. Cam.	
	23.		Lieut. Col. D.A.D. ERVICHE JONES. DSO. MC. mentioned in despatches DATED 18.12.17. 2nd Lt. HAUSLOP rejoined from Hospital. Cam.	
	24.		Lt Col. DERVICHE JONES. D.S.O. MC. resumes command of 2/8 Battalion. Capt. H.W. PRIESTLEY assumes duty as Adjutant. Cam.	
			2nd Lieut. J. M. ELAM posted to A Company Cam.	
do	27.		2nd Lieut D'ARCY proceeded on G.H.Q. Lewis Gun course Cam.	
	28		Lt. Col. D.A. Derviche Jones. D.S.O. M.C. proceeded to CAPE MARTIN on sick leave. Captain H.W. PRIESTLEY Cam	
			assumes command of the Battalion. Lt C.A. MONTGOMERY assumes duties of Adjutant. Cam.	
			Captain E.R. LANES proceeded on leave to England. Cam.	
do	29.		2nd Lieuts McI Brown D.W. LAMB proceeded to 4th Army S.O.S. and Infantry Schools. Cam.	

D. D. & L., London, E.C.
(A7883) Wt. W803/M1672 350,000 4/17 Sch. 52a Forms/C/2118/14

Instructions regarding War Diaries and Intelligence Summaries are contained in F. S. Regs., Part II. and the Staff Manual respectively. Title pages will be prepared in manuscript.

WAR DIARY
or
INTELLIGENCE SUMMARY.
(Erase heading not required.)

Army Form C. 2118.

Place	1917 Date	Hour	Summary of Events and Information	Remarks and references to Appendices
CANAL BANK	DEC 30		Captain KELLY ~~for~~ M.C. proceeded on leave to England. Calm.	
			31 Dec. 1917	
			Hugh W. Prestley Capt. Comᵈ 2/8th London Regt. — C. A. Montgomery Lt. A/Adjutant.	

D. D. & L., London, E.C.
(A7883) Wt. W803/M1672 350,000 4/17 **Sch. 52a** Forms/C/2118/14

Army Form C. 2118.

2/8 London Regt

Vol 13

Instructions regarding War Diaries and Intelligence Summaries are contained in F. S. Regs., Part II. and the Staff Manual respectively. Title pages will be prepared in manuscript.

WAR DIARY
or
INTELLIGENCE SUMMARY.
(Erase heading not required.)

Place	Date	Hour	Summary of Events and Information	Remarks and references to Appendices
	1918 JAN			
CANAL BANK	1		Battalion still on Working Parties. Cam	
"	5		Major A.C. Southern returned from leave + assumed Command of Battalion AWP	
"	6		Lieut C.A. Montgomery went on 14 days leave. AWP.	
"	8	10.30am	The Battalion left Canal Bank B.24.b (Sheet 28)	For Relief Orders see appx A
Road Camp	"	12.30pm	The Battalion arrived at ROAD CAMP (F.25.c. Sheet 27) NEAR St JAN-TER-BIEZEN. AWP	
"	"		Captain T.J. Mumford returned from Musketry Course. AWP	
"	9		2Lt H Booth returned from depot Battalion AWP	
"	10		Captain J.A. Bostock returned from leave. AWP	
"	11		Captain S.R. Lanes returned from leave. AWP	
"	15		Captain C Kelly returned from leave AWP	
"			2Lieut R Sparshot proceeded to England for attachment to M.G. Corps AWP	
"			2Lieut P.F. D'arcy returned from L.G. Course AWP	
			Lieut + QM R.F. Johnson joined for duty AWP	
"	20	1am	The Battalion left ROAD CAMP + proceed via train from PROVEN to new area.	See Appendix B.
MOREUIL		9.45pm	The Battalion Marched into MOREUIL village + was billeted. Detraining station VILLERS BRETONNEUX AWP	

D. D. & L., London, E.C. (A7883) Wt. W803/M1672 350,000 4/17 Sch. 52a Forms/C/2118/14

Instructions regarding War Diaries and Intelligence Summaries are contained in F. S. Regs., Part II. and the Staff Manual respectively. Title pages will be prepared in manuscript.

WAR DIARY
or
INTELLIGENCE SUMMARY.
(Erase heading not required.)

Army Form C. 2118.

Place	Date	Hour	Summary of Events and Information	Remarks and references to Appendices
MOREUIL	Jan 24th		Captain A.D. HEATON proceeded to England to report to India Office for Commission in Indian Army. HWP	
"			Capt J.A. BOSTOCK assumed command of 'A' Coy. HWP	
"			Lieut + QM R.F. Johnson proceeded to PERONNE on Sanitation Course. HWP	
"	25th		2Lieut T. McI BROWN + 2 OR proceeded to forward area - QUIERZY - to reconnoitre + take over billets. HWP	
"			2Lt C.A. Montgomery returned from Leave. HWP	
"	27		Lieut + QM R.F. Johnson returned from Sanitation Course. HWP	
"	30		2Lt Elam proceeded to III Corp Stokes Motar Course HWP	
"			2Lt Carter proceeded to III Corp L.G. Course. HWP	
"		9.45am	The Battalion left MOREUIL HWP } See Appx	"C".
HANGARD		12 noon	The Battalion arrived at HANGARD + was billetted. HWP }	

A. C. Sutton Major
Commanding 2/4th Bn London Regt

D. D. & L., London, E.C.
(A7883) Wt. W803/M1672 350,000 4/17 Sch. 52a Forms/C/2118/14

WAR DIARY

APPDx "A"

SECRET. Copy No:

2/8th Bn., London Regt.

ORDER No: 8. Jan.7th 1918.

Ref. Maps 27 & 28
N.W. 1/20,000

1. The 58th Division is to be relieved by the 35th Division commencing today. On relief the Division is to move to 11 Corps rear area.

2. The battalion will be relieved by the 17th R. Scots tomorrow, Jan. 8th 1918. On relief the battalion will proceed to ROAD CAMP. F.25.c.& d. by train from BOESINGHE Station to PROVEN, thence by march route (In accordance with 1V Army G.S. 148. d/15.12.17, 100 yds will be kept between Coys. and 500 yds bewteen Battalions.)

3. The times of parade and the times of trains will be notified later.

4. 2/Lieut. E.H.Edge will act as entraining officer and will report to Lieut. G.Mills at the entraining station 2 hours before the train starts.

5. The Transport Section will proceed independantly by road under the orders of the Brigade Transport Officer.

6. All defense schemes, track maps etc. and instructions as to actions in case of attack will be handed over to the incoming battalion.

7. The Sapping Platoon under Lieut. A..Moon will return to the battalion at 11. am. today, but will be kept as such antil further orders and will be attached to Bn. H.Q.

8. Os. C. Companies will furnish marching in states within 1 hour of arrival at ROAD CAMP.

9. Attention is drawn to Administrative Instructions issued separately.

10. Anti aircraft posts will be handed over together with mountings issued by 2nd Corps, but anti air-craft sights will be retained and handed over to Sergeant parker.

Hugh W Priestley
Captain & Adjutant.
2/8th Bn. London Regt.

Copy No:
1. C.O.
2. Adjutant.
3. O.C. "A"
4. O.C. "B"
5. O.C. "C"
6. O.C. "D"
7. O.C. H.Q. Section.
8. O.C. Transport.
9. Quartermaster.
10. War Diary.
11. File.

ADMINISTRATIVE INSTRUCTIONS
in connection with Order No: 8.
2/8th Bn., The London Regiment.

Copy No:
7th Jan.

1. Warning Order for move No: 1 dated 6.1.18 holds good except that 1 blanket per man will be carried leaving one only to be conveyed by lorry.

2. The two lorries referred to in Warning Order will report at the Guard Room at 7. a.m. tomorrow.

3. The following apply to H.Q., A. C. & D. Companies
i. One blanket per man will be tightly rolled in bundles of 10 with company lablestied on, and dumped in A. Co. NEISEN HUTS by 6.45. a.m. tomorrow:
ii. Each Company will detail a loading party of 5 men to report to R.Q.M.S. at Bn. Orderly Room at 7. a.m. tomorrow.
iii. Officers kits, Officers mess baskets and O.R. Boxes must be dumped in A. Co. Huts by 7. am. tomorrow.
iv. Dixies kept back for breakfast tomorrow must be cleaned and ready for loading by 7. a.m. tomorrow.
v. Lewis Guns must be ready for loading by 7. am. but will not be loaded prior to the departure of the battalion. If necessary Sergt Parker will remain behind with the L.G.s which will be fetched by a lorry making a second journey.
The following apply to B. Company only.
a. One blanket per man, rolled in bundles of 10 and labled, Officers kits, mess baskets , must be dumped where A.TRACK meets BOESINGHE Rd by 7.30. a.m. tomorrow.
b. The Lewis Guns complete issued for anti air-craft defences will be handed over to Sergt Parker at Bn. H.Q. at 7. a.m. tomorrow.

4. i. Sergt. Owen will arrange for two cooks per company to go with company cookers at 3.30. p.m. today. They will prepare and cook tomorrows dinner which will be consumed on arrival at the new camp.
ii. The Water Duty men (2 per water cart) will procedd with their Water Carts to the new area by road with the Transport Section.

5. The R.Q.M.S. will report at Bn. H.Q. at 7. a.m. tomorrow and will superindent the loading of the lorries.
He will also arrange the following:-
i. The conveyance of Q.M. Stores, bicycles, drums etc. by lorry.
ii. His own loading party from details.
iii. The conveyance of details to the new camp.

6. Os. C. Companies will obtain certificates from their opposite numbers to the effect that billets have been left in a clean and sanitary condition, which will be handed to the Adjutant prior to moving off.

7. Lieut. Shapley for H.Q. and O.C. Companies will return all Soyer Stoves and washing tubs to the Camp Commandant and hand the receipts to the Adjutant rpior to moving off.

contd.

8. Os. C. Companies will report to the Bn. O.R. by 10. am. Jan. 10th that all men detached in this Divisional Area have rejoined. If not state what parties are still away.

9. Rations for consumption on the 9th will be delivered in the new area.

10. Railhead will be PESELHOEK from 9.1.18.

Hugh W. Priestley

Captain & Adjutant.
2/8th Bn., London Regiment.

Copies to R.S.M. and all recepients of Order No: 8.

War diary

APPx B

S E C R E T.

Os. C. Companies.
Headquarters.
Transport Officer.
Quartermaster.
Lieut. A. Moon.

---

1. Reference Warning Order of yesterday, the advance party consisting of Lieut. A. MOON, his batman, H.Q. and Co. CQMS.s. and N.C.O. from the Transport Section (1 Officer 7 O.Rks) will parade outside Bn. Orderly Room at 3.45. a.m. tomorrow ready to proceed to POPERINGHE Station.

2. The train leaves POPERINGHE Station at 6.15. a.m. and Lt.MOON will report to Lieut. HARRISON-JONES at 4.45. a.m. at that Station.

3. Captain T.A.B.PURKIS will travel with the advance party and will be responsible for transport accommodation in the new area. His batman will be attached to the Bn. Advance Party for the journey.

4. The Quartermaster will dump 4 days rations for 2 Officers and 8 Other Ranks in sandbags in the Orderly Room by 3. a.m. tomorrow Jan. 16th.

5. The Transport Officer will detail a limber to report to Bn. Orderly Room at 3.45. a.m. tomorrow to carry officers and Other Ranks kits and rations to Bde H.Q. where they will be transferred to transport arranged by Brigade. The limber must report at Brigade by 4. a.m.

6. 2 blankets per O.Rk. will be taken, one strapped on the back of the pack, the other rolled beneath the pack.

7. Lieut. A.MOON will obtain a movement order for 1 Officer and 8 Other Ranks from the Bn. O.R. before starting.
Captain T.A.B.PURKIS's movement order will be issued by Bde HQ.

8. The party will be marched to POPERINGHE Station in rear of the Transport under the senior N.C.O. and report to Lieut.MOON.

9. Detraining Station VILLERS BRETONNEUX and the probable time of arrival is 11.30. p.m. January 16th.

HUGH. W. PRIESTLEY.
Captain & Adjutant.

15. 1. 18.

Issued to Signals at 8. 45. p.m.

S E C R E T. Copy No: 10

ENTRAINMENT INSTRUCTIONS No.?

of [illegible] Bn. London Regt. Move to Fifth Army.

---

1. The battalion will complete the departure of the 17[illegible] Brigade group and will leave [illegible] STATION at [illegible] a.m. on Sunday Jan. [illegible] arriving VILLERS - BRETONNEUX at [illegible] the same day.

2. (a) 2/Lieut. [illegible] D'Arcy will act as Bn. Entraining Officer & will report to Captain [illegible], H.Q. [illegible] Bn (Brigade Entraining Officer) at [illegible] a.m. Jan. [illegible]. He will hand in the the Bn. Entraining State in triplicate to the Bde. Entraining Officer's clerk [illegible] office half an hour previous to arrival of the Battalion at the Station.

(b) A. & B. Companies will each detail [illegible] Officers and [illegible] platoons [illegible] Officers and [illegible] Other Ranks to act as loading party. They will parade at Bn. Parade Ground at [illegible] p.m. Jan. [illegible]th and will be marched by the Senior Officer to [illegible] Station reporting to the [illegible] at [illegible] midnight Jan [illegible].

(c) C. Company ([illegible] Officers & [illegible] Other Ranks) will act as unloading party at VILLERS BRETONNEUX.

O.C. C. Company will report to Lieut. [illegible] (Brigade Detraining Officer) for instructions immediately on arrival.

3. (a) The Transport Section complete with supply and baggage wagons will arrive at [illegible] STATION at [illegible] a.m. Jan. 19th. All vehicles must be loaded by [illegible] a.m. Jan. [illegible]th.

(b) The battalion will arrive at [illegible] STATION at [illegible] a.m. Jan [illegible]th.

4. The composition of the train will be:-
   - [illegible] covered wagons.
   - 17 flats.
   - 1 officers coach.

5. [illegible] Baggage and [illegible] wagons will report to these H.Q. during the afternoon of Jan [illegible]th.

6. Special instructions with reference to supplies will be issued later.

7. Water Carts will be filled from the stand pipes at the Station prior to being entrained.

The T.O. should endeavour to obtain some [illegible] gallon petrol cans to [illegible] take in the horse trucks.

A halt of 1 hour will be made at [illegible].

8. Instructions as to [illegible] will be issued later.

[illegible],
Captain & Adjutant.

[illegible].1.18.

Copy No: 1 War Diary.
2 H.Q.
3 A. Company.
5 C. Company.
6 D. Company.
7 [illegible].

SECRET

Copy No 1

TRANSPORT ORDERS in connection
ADMINISTRATIVE INSTRUCTIONS No: 9 for
Move to Fifth Army. Jan. 17th.

---

1. Transport will draw up on the platform from North End into double column - limbers, cookers etc. being kept together - opposite the Flats.
The platform at PROVEN is sufficiently long 29 trucks to be loaded simultaneously.

2. On arrival at Station.
   (a) Transport Officer will detail 2 men to fill the water trough.
   (b) Transport Officer will detail 1 N.C.O. and 6 men to report to Brigade Transport Officer with the head ropes for horse trucks.
   (c) Animals will be unhooked and led away to water.
   (d) On returning from watering, animals will be lined up opposite the trucks allotted to them. All harness and men's equipment will be taken off and stacked on the side of platform away from the train, before commencing to entrain.

3. Endeavour must be made to procure 4 gallon petrol yins which will be filled at Station and taken into horse trucks. Failing this all available 2 gallon tins will be filled.

4. Water Carts are to be entrained full, they are to be filled before leaving camp and not as stated in para 7 of Administrative Orders No 9

5. Four water buckets to be taken into each horse truck.

6. Hay nets should be filled before moving off and given to animals when in the trucks. Nose bags should contain two feeds.

OVERLEAF
7.

7. Transport Cooks should take dixies into their wagons. Hot water for tea should be procured at ABBEVILLE.

8. There is a hut at the Station where biscuits, chocolate etc may be bought. No man is to leave the platform without permission.

HUGH W. PRIESTLEY,
Captain & Adjutant.

Copy No: 1. War Diary.
2 C.O.
3. Q.M.
4. Transport Sergt.
5. " N.C.O.
6. " N.C.O.
7. " N.C.O.

Issued to Signals at 10. a.m. 17. 1. 18.

SECRET.

Copy No. /

2/8th Bn. The London Regiment.
ORDER NO: 9.

Ref: Map Sheet 27
Belgium & France
AMIENS 1.100,000.

Jan. 18th.

---

1. The battalion will move by rail to the new area in accordance with Administrative Orders No.9 and Transport Orders already issued.

2. The Battalion will leave the Camp for PROVEN Station in the following order: H.Q., D. C. B. A.
Starting Point: Battalion Orderly Room.
The head of the column will pass the starting point at 1 am January 20th. Watches to be synchronised at Bn.O.R. at 12.45 am.

3. Route: To PROVEN via Cross Roads in F.25.c. turning to the right at Cross Roads in F.12.d.

4. Dress: Full marching order with 1 blanket rolled in ground sheet and strapped on back of the pack. Soft caps will be worn and steel helmets at back of pack.
Rations for Jan.20th will be carried on the man.
Water bottles must be full.

5. The following stores etc. must be dumped, ready to be loaded on lorries, outside Battalion Orderly Room by 9.30 am Jan.19th -
   - Signal Stores.
   - Transport Stores.
   - Orderly Room Stores.
   - Canteen Stores.
   - Surplus M.O.'s Stores.
   - 1 blanket per man in bundles of 10 and labelled.
   - Tailors and shoemakers stores
   - Surplus Officers Mess Stores.

6. Loading Party: from D. Company.
   i. A loading party of 40 Other Ranks to include 2 good N.C.O.s to report to Q.M. at 10 am Jan.19th.
   ii. A loading party of 1 Officer and 40 Other Ranks to be at PROVEN Station at 10.30 am ready to unload the lorries as they arrive.
   iii. A guard of 1 N.C.O. and 3 Other Ranks with rations for Jan. 19th and 20th to be at PROVEN Station at 10.30 am ready to guard the stores dumped by the lorries.
   This guard will entrain with its company.

7. The following will be the loading arrangements on Jan.19th.
The M.O.s Cart will report at M.O. Hut and be loaded at 3 pm.
L.G.s limbers and S.A.A. limbers will be loaded at Transport lines by 3 pm.
Tool limbers will report at Q.M. Stores at 3 pm for loading.
Water Carts will be filled and ready to proceed to Transport Lines by 3.30 pm.
Cookers and Officers Mess Cart will be loaded and ready to move off at 10 pm.
Officers Kits will be at Q.M. Stores by 3.30 pm.
All petrol cans to be returned to the Q.M. Store by 2 pm.

contd.
para 8.

8. The sick will parade under arrangements to be made by M.O. at 11.30 pm Jan.19th and will be marched by the Medical Corporal to PROVEN STATION and await the Battalion.

9. Each Company and H.Q. will leave a rear party of 1 N.C.O. and 6 men behind to ensure their lines are left clean and tidy. Captain MUMFORD will also remain behind and will be in charge of these parties. After obtaining a certificate from the Camp Adjutant that the camp is clean he will march these parties to PROVEN Station to join the Battalion.
The Transport Sergeant will be responsible for the cleanliness of the Transport lines.

10. O.C. Companies will arrange to have a half ration of tea issued at 4.30 pm on Jan.19th and a final meat tea about 7.30 pm.

11. 3 lorries for taking stores to PROVEN Station will be available after the 2/6th Battalion have finished with them on Jan.19th. The Q.M. will get in touch with the 2/6th Bn and will provide guides to report to the 2/6th Bn to travel on the lorries and bring them back to this Bn.H.Q. He will also be responsible for seeing that these lorries are dismissed by 3.0 pm Jan.19th, and for obtaining a statement from each driver showing at what hour they were dismissed.

12. Ref. para 2 (c) of ADMINISTRATIVE INSTRUCTIONS No. 9.
O.C. C Company will tell off his company as an unloading party as follows:
(a) 1 Officer 60 Other Ranks for unloading vehicles.
(b) 1 Officer 40 Other Ranks for unloading Q.M. Stores.

13. Ref. para 7 of ADMINISTRATIVE INSTRUCTIONS No. 9. for <u>ABBEVILLE</u> read <u>TINQUES</u> about 7 hours journey from PROVEN.

14. The battalion will probably be billeted at MOREUIL, 7 miles from VILLERS BRETONNEUX.

15. String and labels must be carried in case the blanket carried on the man can be dumped at the detraining station and be carried on lorries.

HUGH W. PRIESTLEY,
Captain & Adjutant.

Issued at 3.45 pm Jan. 18th.

Copies No. 1. War Diary.
2. C.O.
3. H.Q.
4. A Co.
5. B Co.
6. C Co.
7. D Co.
8. Transport.
9. Quartermaster.
10. Adjutant.
11. File.

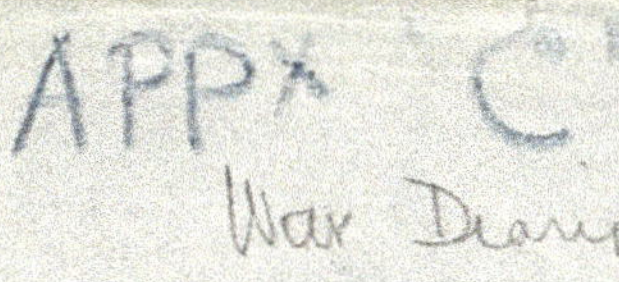

SECRET. Copy No: 2

2/8th London Regt Order No:10.

Ref: Map Sheet 66 E
1/40000. 29. 1. 18.

---

1. Units of the 174th Brigade Group now billeted in MOREUIL and MORISEL will move tomorrow, Jan 30th. by march route to billets as under.
Present billets to be clear by 3. p.m.

Brigade & 5th Londons.	BERTEAUCOURT.
7th Londons.	DOMART.
8th Londons.	HANGARD.
2/2nd H.C.F.A.	LES-PINOY FARM.
511th H.T. Co. A.S.C.	HOURGES.

2. ROUTE: THENNES - BERTEAUCOURT - DOMART.

3. Starting Point: Map ref. B.26.d.2.1.

4.

Order of March	Time of passing starting point.
511th A.S.C.	9.50. a.m.
8th Londons.	10. 0. a.m.
7th Londons.	10.15. a.m.
5th Londons.	10.30. a.m.
Brigade H.Q.	10.35. a.m.

Transport will accompany units.

5. The Battalion will parade at 9.45. a.m. in THIBAUVILLE RD. in column of route, facing N.W. in the follwoing order:
Band.
A. Company.
B. Company.
C. Company.
D. Company.
H.Q.
Transport.
With the head of the column at junction of road at point I.2.b.2.6.

6. DRESS: Full marching order, with one blanket rolled in ground sheet carried on top of the pack. Steel helmets will be worn.

7 Lieut. A.Moon and C.Q.M.S.s. will proceed in advance leving present Bn. H.Q. at 8. a.m.

8. Marching out states will be handed into Bn. O.R. at 9. a.m. Marching in States within an hour of arrival at new area.

9. ACKNOWLEDGE.

HUGH.W.PRIESTLEY.
Captain & Adjutant.

Issued to Sigs at 4.45.p.m.
Copies to
1. C.O.
2. Adjutant.
3. O.C. "A"
4. O.C. "B"
5. O.C. "C"
6. O.C. "D"
7. Headquarters.
8. T.O.
9. Q.M.

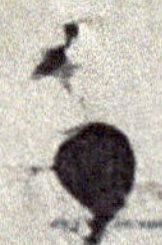

ADMINISTRATIVE ORDERS in
connection with ORDER No: 18. 29. 1. 18.

---

1. Baggage wagons will report today and will be parked in VICTOR HUGO Square.
Horses will be returned to 511th Co. A.S.C. for the night. and will report at 7. a.m. tomorrow the 30th inst.

2. The T.O. and Q.M. will arrange to transport as much of the Q.M. Store as possible to new area today.
O.C. B. Compant has been detailed to supply a guard of 1. N.C.O. and 4. men to proceed with these stores.

3. Supplies for 31st inst will be delivered to Q.M. Store in new area by 4. p.m. tomorrow. The Q.M. will send a guide to be at the refilling point on AMIENS - ROYE Road at HOURGE O.3.b.8.9. to arrive there at 3. 9. p.m. tomorrow.

4. The following articles and stores will be dumped under the direction of the R.S.M. in VICTOR HUGO Square at 7.30.am. tomorrow
   Signalling Stores.
   Orderly Room Stores.
   Canteen Stores.
   M.O.s. Stores.
   Surplus Mess Stores.
   1 blanket per man in bundles of 10 securely tied and labelled.
   Q.M.Stores.

5. Officers kits will be dumped at the same place at 8. a.m.
The Mess Cart will report at H.Q.Mess at 9. a.m.
Company Mess Boxes to be dumped outside H.Q.Mess at 9. a.m

6. O.C. A. Company will detail a loading party of 2 N.C.O.s. and 20 men to report to R.S.M. at VICTOR HUGO Square at 7.30. am. and will also detail a similar party to report to Q.M. Store for unloading immediately on arrival at HAMHARD.

7. All billets will be left clean and tidy.
Lieut. T.J. Mumford will inspect billets between 8.30. am. and 9. 30. .am. and will obtain a certificate from the Aera Commandant to the effect that they have been left in a clean state.

HUGH.W.PRIESTLEY.
Captain & Adjutant.

Copies to all receipients of ORDER No:19.

Army Form C. 2118.

8 London

Vol 14

Instructions regarding War Diaries and Intelligence Summaries are contained in F. S. Regs., Part II. and the Staff Manual respectively. Title pages will be prepared in manuscript.

WAR DIARY or INTELLIGENCE SUMMARY.

(Erase heading not required.)

Place	Date	Hour	Summary of Events and Information	Remarks and references to Appendices
HANGARD	Feb 1		Lieut P.C. Darcy proceeded on a transport Course. HWP	
"			Lieut A Moon proceeded to 174th Bde as Intelligence Officer (temporarily) HWP	
	2		6 Officers 161 OR of 1/8th Battalion London Regt joined 2/8th Battalion. Officers names – T/Lieut Col WB Vince, T/Capt JEB Jacob, Captain HH King, Lieut LA Malleson, Lieut EC Krell, Lieut L J Howes (13th Londons). HWP	
	3		2/Lieut H. Booth + 2/Lieut D F Wilkinson went on leave	
			Lieut DW Lamb returned from course. HWP	
	5		Lieut C G Potter reported for duty from 1/8 Battalion HWP	
	8	6am	The Battalion left HANGARD, entrained at VILLERS BRETONNEUX detrained at APPILLY and bussed to HQ, A+B Coys to PIERREMANDE, C+D Coys to AUTREVILLE and relieved 2nd Bn BEDFORDSHIRE REGT. at 5.15pm. See Appx 'A' HWP	
			Lieut Col A.D. DERVICHE-JONES DSO MC rejoined the Battalion from Sick Leave. HWP	
PIERREMANDE	9	9.45pm	The Battalion relieved 2nd Bn Royal Scots Fusiliers in BARISIS Sector, Right	
BARISIS			Subsector of 58th Division III Corps. Dispositions + Relief orders are shown in Appx 'B' HWP	
	10		Very quiet.	
	12		Capt + Adjt L E B Jacob, Lieut + QM R.F. Johnson, RQMS Brand, Sergt Goshawke + Sergt Owen proceeded to III Corps Reinforcement HWP	

D. D. & L., London, E.C. (A7883) Wt. W803/M1672 350,000 4/17 Sch. 52a Forms/C/2118/14

Instructions regarding War Diaries and Intelligence Summaries are contained in F. S. Regs., Part II. and the Staff Manual respectively. Title pages will be prepared in manuscript.

Army Form C. 2118.

WAR DIARY
or
INTELLIGENCE SUMMARY.
(Erase heading not required.)

Place	Date	Hour	Summary of Events and Information	Remarks and references to Appendices
			Camp as surplus on amalgamation HWP.	
	14		Capt J.A. Bostock returned from L.G. Course HWP	
			2/Lieut P.C. D'arcy returned from Transport Course HWP	
	15		Captain R. Fairley MC reported for duty from leave. HWP Reinforcements 39 O.R. joined 8th Bn.	
	16		2/Lieut Briggsmeyer returned to continue Div Signal Course. HWP	
			Lieut Col A.D. Derviche-Jones DSO MC. left the line to go on a Flying Course HWP	
	17		2/Lieut J.E. ELAM rejoined from T M Course HWP	
			Lieut R.J.F. Carter rejoined from L.G. Course. HWP	
	18		2/Lieut J.E. ELAM attached to 174 T M Battery. HWP	
			Capt C Kelley proceeded to III Corps Gas Course. HWP	
	20		Capt + Adjt H.W. Priestley proceeded on special leave HWP	
			Lt C.G. Potter assumed duties of acting Adjutant HWP	
	21		Capt J.A. Bostock proceeded to England for commission in Indian Army HWP	
	22		Reinforcements of 10 O.R. joined Bn HWP Lt Col A.D. Derviche Jones rejoined Bn HWP	
	24		2nd Lt L.J. Howes proceeded on 5th Army Musketry course HWP	
	25		Reinforcements 12 officers and 39 O.R. joined Bn. See appendix "B"	

D. D. & L., London, E.C.
(A7883) Wt. W800/M1672 350,000 4/17 Sch. 52a Forms/C2118/14

Army Form C. 2118.

Instructions regarding War Diaries and Intelligence Summaries are contained in F. S. Regs., Part II. and the Staff Manual respectively. Title pages will be prepared in manuscript.

WAR DIARY
or
INTELLIGENCE SUMMARY.

(Erase heading not required.)

Place	Date	Hour	Summary of Events and Information	Remarks and references to Appendices
BARISIS	Feb 26		Capt H.H KING left to take up duties as area commandant, SINCENY	[initials]
	27		2nd Lt E.H. EDGE proceeded on leave to U.K. [initials]	
	28		8th Bn took over part of the front held by 6th Bn London Regt, up to & including ROUTE CHALATTE [initials].	
			2nd Lts BOOTH & LOCKE proceeded on III Corps Infantry Course [initials]	
			Total Casualties during month 2 OR killed, 1 OR wounded [initials]	

[signature]
Major
Cmdg 8th London Regt

D. D. & L., London, E.C.
(A7883) Wt. W809/M1672 350,000 4/17 Sch. 52a Forms/C/2118/14

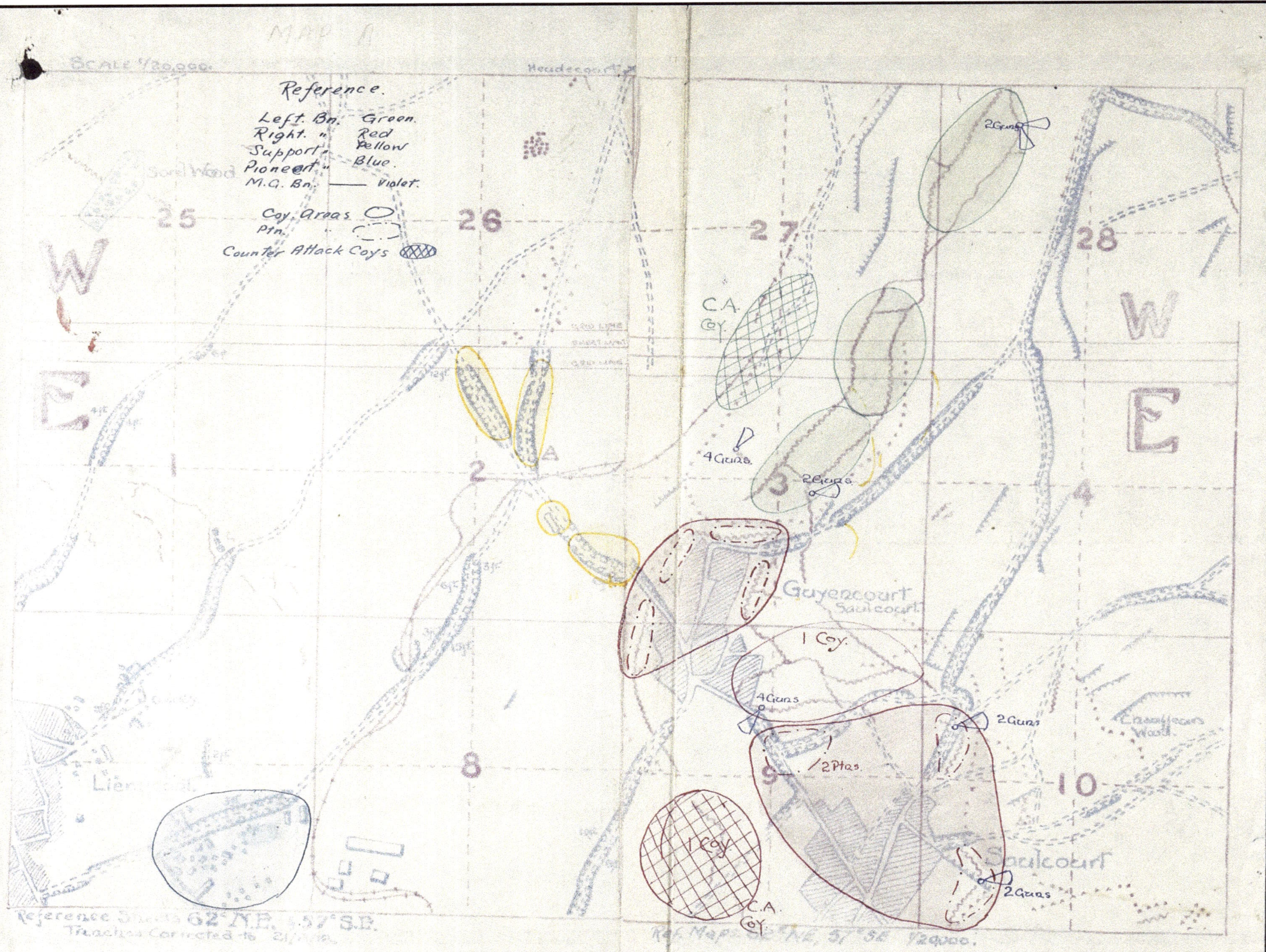

MAP A
SCALE 1/20,000
Reference.
Left Bn. Green.
Right. " Red
Support " Yellow
Pioneer " Blue.
M.G. Bn. —— Violet.
Coy Areas
Ptn.
Counter Attack Coys
Headecourt
25
26
27
28
W
E
1
2
3
4
8
9
10
A
C.A. Coy.
4 Guns.
2 Guns.
1 Coy.
2 Ptns.
Guyencourt
Saulcourt
Saulcourt
Reference Sheets 62^c N.E. & 57^c S.E.
Ref. Maps 62^c N.E. 57^c S.E. 1/20000.

www.ingramcontent.com/pod-product-compliance
Lightning Source LLC
Chambersburg PA
CBHW081434160426
43193CB00013B/2278

* 9 7 8 1 4 7 4 5 3 1 3 9 9 *